MathLinks

Activities Connecting School and Home

Kindergarten

Laurel Robertson

Lisa Borah

Camilla Schneider

Megan Weber

Developmental Studies Center
2000 Embarcadero, Suite 305
Oakland, CA 94606

Developmental Studies Center
2000 Embarcadero, Suite 305
Oakland, CA 94606
(510) 533-0213, (800) 666-7270
www.devstu.org

This project was supported by the National Science Foundation under grant no. ESI-9705421. Opinions expressed are those of the authors and not necessarily those of the Foundation.

The project also was supported by the Ewing Marion Kauffman Foundation under strategic grant no. 20000853.

MathLinks was developed by the Home, School, and Community Project, a program of the Developmental Studies Center, 2000 Embarcadero, Suite 305, Oakland, California 94606.

Design: Kathleen Cunningham
Illustrations: Dave Garbot
Cover Design: Kathleen Cunningham
Composition: Leigh McLellan

ISBN 1-57621-362-5

Funding to support the development, piloting, and dissemination of Developmental Studies Center programs has been provided by:

The Annenberg Foundation, Inc.
Anonymous Donor
The Robert Bowne Foundation, Inc.
The Annie E. Casey Foundation
Center for Substance Abuse Prevention
Substance Abuse and Mental Health Services Agency
U.S. Department of Health and Human Services
The Danforth Foundation
The DuBarry Foundation
The Ford Foundation
Evelyn and Walter Haas, Jr. Fund
J. David & Pamela Hakman
Family Foundation
Hasbro Children's Foundation
Charles Hayden Foundation
The William Randolph Hearst Foundation
Clarence E. Heller Charitable Foundation
The William and Flora Hewlett Foundation
The James Irvine Foundation
The Robert Wood Johnson Foundation
Walter S. Johnson Foundation
Ewing Marion Kauffman Foundation
W.K. Kellogg Foundation
John S. and James L. Knight Foundation
Lilly Endowment, Inc.
The MBK Foundation
Mr. & Mrs. Sanford N. McDonnell
The John D. and Catherine T. MacArthur Foundation
A.L. Mailman Family Foundation, Inc.
Charles Stewart Mott Foundation
National Institute on Drug Abuse (NIDA), National Institutes of Health
National Science Foundation
Nippon Life Insurance Foundation
The Pew Charitable Trusts
The Pinkerton Foundation
The Rockefeller Foundation
Louise and Claude Rosenberg, Jr.
The San Francisco Foundation
Shinnyo-En Foundation
Silver Giving Foundation
The Spencer Foundation
Spunk Fund, Inc.
Stuart Foundation
The Stupski Family Foundation
The Sulzberger Foundation, Inc.
Surdna Foundation, Inc.
U.S. Department of Education
Wallace-Reader's Digest Funds
Wells Fargo Bank

Contents

ACKNOWLEDGMENTS

Many people were involved in the development and production of **MathLinks**. We are grateful for their time, valuable suggestions, and encouragement.

We wish to express our deep appreciation to the National Science Foundation and to the Ewing Marion Kauffman Foundation and, in particular, to our program officers, John "Spud" Bradley and Margo Quiriconi for their support.

We also wish to thank the teachers, principals, parents, youth development, and education leaders who served on our Advisory Board:

Louise Bevilaqua

Ginny Bolin

Nancy Bowen

Sandra Casares

Ronald Cooper

Sue Eldredge

Gilberto Guerrero, Jr.

Sue Hymel

Michael McAfee

Ginnie Miller

Georgina Peraza

Carol Price

June Robinson

Dan Safran

Carter Savage

Beth Skipper

Virginia Thompson

Gail Vessels

Philip Wagreich

We wish to thank the following people who advised the developers and contributed enormously to the development of the program:

Susie Alldredge

Julie Contestable

Mary Euretig

Norman Ferrer

José Luis Franco

Carol Inzerillo

Pablo Jasis

Constance Kamii

Kelly Killam

Socorro Lara

John Mergendoller

Jan Mokros

Megan Murray

Leona Peters

Alma Ramirez

Glenn Singleton

Many teachers field-tested the activities, allowed us in their classrooms to observe, and provided us with feedback that helped shape the content and format of the program. We particularly wish to acknowledge the principals, teachers, parents, and children from the following schools:

California

Oakland Unified School District

- Hawthorne Elementary School

Burlingame School District

- Lincoln School
- Washington Elementary School

San Francisco Unified School District

- Jean Parker Elementary School

Louisiana

East Baton Rouge Parish School System

- Dalton Elementary
- Jefferson Terrace Elementary
- Tanglewood Elementary

Missouri

Kansas City, Missouri School District

- James Elementary School
- J.S. Chick African Centered Elementary School
- William A. Knotts Environmental Studies Magnet School

MathLinks

We thank the principals, teachers, parents, and children from the following California school districts who allowed the authors to pilot the **MathLinks** activities in their classrooms and homes:

Alameda Unified School District

Berkeley Unified School District

Hayward Unified School District

Jefferson Elementary School District

Mt. Diablo Unified School District

Oakland Unified School District

San Francisco Unified School District

San Rafael City Schools

We also thank the past and present staff of the Developmental Studies Center, particularly the following people, for their support:

Eric Schaps, President

Judy Kingsley, Managing Director

Frank Snyder, Executive Vice President

Pam Herrera, Director of Administration

Dimi Berkner, Marketing Director

Sherry Jacobs Stover, Accountant Manager

Finally, the publication of this book would not have been possible without the help of other **MathLinks** staff and contributors:

Cindy Stephens, Assistant Project Director

Muriel Christianson, Administrative Assistant/Proofreader

Rosalie Torres, Director of Research and Evaluation

Victor Battistich, Deputy Director of Research

Ann House, Research Associate

Julie Duff, Research Associate

Elvia Teixeira, Curriculum Developer

Kathleen Cunningham, Design

Dave Garbot, Illustration

Amy Bauman, Editor

Mary Fraser, Editor

Leigh McLellan, Production

Welcome to MATHLINKS!

Making links in their thinking and lives helps children learn. **MathLinks** provides opportunities for children to make such links by connecting their learning at school with their learning at home. As children explore and discuss mathematics with their parents (or other significant older person in their lives) they deepen their understanding, enjoyment, and sense of connection to mathematics.

MathLinks also links children's mathematical and social learning. As children work with others at home and at school, they learn the skills needed to work together successfully and communicate effectively. They also learn to take responsibility for their learning and behavior.

You will benefit from these connections as well. Through the comments on the activities written to you by children and parents and through class discussion of the home activities, you gain insights into children's learning experiences at home. You learn about their successes and problems with the mathematics and how parents perceive their children's skills. You also learn how families extend or change the home activities with their children.

These enjoyable **MathLinks** activities will give your children more practice with the skills and concepts in your curriculum. They will help your children learn to work with others and be responsible. They also will help parents understand more about the mathematics that their children are learning and how to help their children at home.

We hope you enjoy them!

Laurel Robertson
Lisa Borah
Camilla Schneider
Megan Weber

Using MATHLINKS

MathLinks for kindergarten includes three sets of activities: number, measurement, and geometry. The number set includes an overview and six activities. The measurement and geometry sets each include an overview and three activities.

The Overviews

Each set of activities begins with an overview that provides information to help you use them. Reading the overview before beginning the activities will help you understand how they fit with your curriculum and meet your children's needs. Each activity in the set is summarized for you. Information is provided about the mathematical and social skills and concepts that the activities help children develop. These skills and concepts also are presented in quick reference charts. At the end of each overview you will find an annotated list of children's literature books that you might use with the activities.

☛ *Hint from a MathLinks Teacher:* I read all of the overviews at the beginning of the year to decide where the MathLinks activities will best fit with my curriculum.

The Activities

Each **MathLinks** activity has three related parts; an introductory activity titled **At School**, a home activity titled **At Home**, and a follow-up activity titled **Back at School**.

At School

The **At School** activity involves children in an exploration or game that extends their experience with the mathematical concepts in your curriculum and prepares them for the activity that they will do at home. The **At School** activity has several sections: *Get Ready, Make Connections, Explain and Model the Game/Activity, Pair Work, Report and Reflect,* and *Prepare for Success at Home.*

Get Ready lists the materials that you will need for the activity and may suggest related children's literature that you might use to introduce the activity.

☛ *Hint from a MathLinks Teacher:* The materials needed for the activities are not a problem as they are things you probably have in your classroom. What is important is to prepare them in advance.

Make Connections helps you connect the **At School** activity to your classroom curriculum, to other **MathLinks** activities, and to your children's lives. Here, as throughout **MathLinks**, open-ended questions are suggested (in English and in Spanish) to help you promote your children's mathematical thinking and support their ability to work together effectively. These questions are intended as suggestions only. Note that some of the questions include brackets; for example: "How many of these paper strips tall is [Josie]?" "How do you know that your [mirror] is about as tall as I am?" The words in the brackets are examples; you should fill in the names or terms appropriate for your class.

☛ *Hint from a MathLinks Teacher:*
I read the activity before using it
and circle the questions I want to
ask or write in other questions.

Explain and Model the Game/Activity gives
directions for the activity and suggests
ways to demonstrate it for the entire class
before children begin their pair or group
work. **MathLinks** recommends that you
model the activity or game with a child as
your partner or have a pair of children
model it for the class. This modeling not
only helps children understand the activity, but also provides opportunities to discuss how pairs might work together and
the mathematics they will explore.

☛ *Hint from a MathLinks Teacher:*
I had never modeled an activity
before using MathLinks. It is a very
effective way to help children understand the task and think about how
to work with a partner. With my
kindergartners, I sometimes model
an activity more than once.

Pair Work suggests ways for you to support children as they do the activity or
play the game. Sample open-ended questions are provided to ask pairs about their
work, their thinking, and how they are
working together. This is a great time for
you to do some informal assessment
regarding children's mathematical thinking and ability to work with others.

☛ *Hint from a MathLinks Teacher:*
Children need some experience
working with a partner before
beginning these activities. My children also are more successful if
we do some class building or team
building activities first.

Report and Reflect provides a time for pairs
to share their work, reflection about how
pairs worked together, and further class
discussion about the mathematics explored. Frequently, **MathLinks** suggests
that discussion be conducted first in pairs
and then as a class. Accompanying
Teacher Tips may recommend a cooperative strategy to facilitate the pair discussion. (Cooperative strategies are
suggested at other times in the activity as
well. See *Sharing in Pairs,* p. 20, for information about these strategies.)

☛ *Hint from a MathLinks Teacher:*
My children learn so much from
each other when they hear what
other pairs did and we discuss the
activity and the math as a class.

☛ *Hint from a MathLinks Teacher:*
After an activity, talking about
how they worked together, what
went well and, especially, what
didn't, helps children get better at
working with a partner.

Also included in the **At School** activity is
a section titled *Prepare for Success at Home*.
Young children need support as they
learn to be responsible for home activities.
Prepare for Success at Home helps children
understand the **At Home** activity, their
responsibilities for the activity, and some
strategies to help them be responsible.
This section also helps children understand how the work they do at home will
be used in the **Back at School** activity.

To help children be successful:
• Preview the **At Home** activity with the
  class. You might role play the activity,
  particularly if your children are from
  low-literate or limited-English families.

- Help children think about whom they might ask to be a home partner, when is a good time to ask, and what they might do if they have problems finding a home partner.

- Talk about the materials children and their home partners might use for the activity.

- Explain when the home activities need to be returned and what children will do in the **Back at School** activity.

- Help children think about how to remember to bring their work back to school and why it is important.

☞ *Hint from a MathLinks Teacher:*
I either do the Prepare for Success at Home right after the At School activity or at the end of the day. If do it with the At School activity, at the end of the day I briefly remind children about their responsibilities.

At Home

Children work with a home partner to complete the **At Home** activity. The home partner is a learning partner who engages in the activity with the child. This may be an unfamiliar role for some parents. Most parents are accustomed to teaching skills to their children, such as how to count, and to checking their children's homework. The **At Home** activities involve parents in a different role—as active partners in the activity, exploring and discussing the activity and mathematics with their child rather than just monitoring what they do or quizzing them on what they know. Although it is desirable that the home partner is the child's parent, the home partner can be any significant older person, including a brother or sister, aunt, grandparent, neighbor, or family friend.

☞ *Hint from a MathLinks Teacher:*
I had my children make Family Trees to help them think about who could be a home partner. We also made Friend Trees and Neighbor Trees.

☞ *Hint from a MathLinks Teacher:*
If children cannot find a home partner, suggest that they ask someone in their after-school or extended-day program to help them. Or have them work with an aide, a resource teacher, the custodian, the school secretary, an older child at school, or even someone in the class who did the activity.

The **At Home** activity begins with a letter that describes the mathematics the class is exploring, some mathematical vocabulary children are learning, and the activity the child and home partner will do together. Following the letter, the materials needed for the activity are listed, with alternative materials suggested. The activity is presented, with helpful illustrations. A recording space is provided, as is a place for the child and home partner to write a letter to the teacher about the activity. Finally, discussion questions are suggested that will help the child get ready to talk about the activity with others at school and help them think about what needs to go back to school and how to get it there.

☞ *Hint from a MathLinks Teacher:*
Send home the At Home activity
in a special folder that is just for
MathLinks. Colored plastic folders
with ties work really well and last
for the whole year.

Back at School

The **Back at School** activity allows children, with a partner and as a class, to share and discuss their experiences with the **At Home** activity. Children might organize and analyze the data from home and/or explore a follow-up activity. Extension activities for another day are suggested in a section titled *Extend the Experience*.

Prior to doing the **Back at School** activity, review the information that children and their home partners recorded on the **At Home** activity. This will help you determine the mathematical questions to discuss with the class and give you information about how individual children, and the class as a whole, approached the activity. It also will help you determine whether children need further experiences with the mathematical concepts and the extension activities that might provide these experiences.

☞ *Hint from a MathLinks Teacher:*
The Back at School activity is a
real motivator for my children to
return their At Home activities.
They want to talk about what they
did at home and have this information used in a class activity.

☞ *Hint from a MathLinks Teacher:*
I ask for the At Home activities to
be returned at least a day before
I plan to do the Back at School
activity. This gives me time to look
at them before we do the activity
and gives an extra day for children
who forget them on the due date
to return them in time to do the
activity.

Additional Information

Each activity includes other information to help you: class arrangement icons, game directions, and teacher tips.

Children Working in Pairs

Whole Class

Whole Class in Pairs

Located next to most sections of the activity are class arrangement icons. A quick glance at these icons will tell you the suggested class arrangement for that part of the activity: whole class, whole class with children in assigned pairs, or pairs working individually.

To make it easier to find and read them, directions for each game are provided in a games directions box next to the *Explain and Model the Game* section.

Finally, scattered throughout the activity are "Teacher Tips" that provide helpful suggestions, background information, or suggestions for cooperative strategies to use at that point in the activity.

When to Use MathLinks

The **MathLinks** activities are intended to be used when similar concepts are introduced in the classroom to give children more experience with those concepts. You may, however, decide to use the activities as a way to review concepts later in the year. The content of your curriculum and the readiness of your class are the most important factors in determining which **MathLinks** activities to use and when. The number, measurement, and geometry sets may be used in any order. As the mathematical and group work skills build from activity to activity within each set, it is suggested that you implement the activities in a set in the order that they are presented.

Many kindergarten teachers wait to use the **MathLinks** activities until children have a few months of school experience. If you wish to use them earlier in the year, review the mathematics, social skills, and cooperative work in the activities to determine if the activities are appropriate or need some modification.

Most families need several days to complete each activity, so **MathLinks** suggests that you send home no more than one activity per week.

☛ *Hint from a MathLinks Teacher:*
I experiment until I find out when it's best to send home the At Home activities. For some classes, sending it home for families to do over the weekend is best. For others, it works best to send it home on Monday and ask for it back on Thursday or Friday.

Materials Needed

MathLinks was designed to require as few materials and as little preparation as possible for you and for families. The materials needed for all of the **At School** and **Back at School** activities are listed below. Each **MathLinks** activity also lists the materials needed for that activity. Blackline masters are included with each activity.

While the Literature Link suggestions are optional, the books recommended for use with the activities are listed below after the materials for each activity.

For all of the activities, you will need a chalkboard, whiteboard, chart paper or overhead projector. You also will need chalk, marking pens, or overhead pens. Children will need access to crayons or marking pens, scissors, tape, staplers, glue, pencils, and sheets of paper. As these materials need to be available for all of the activities, they are not listed below.

Number 1 Matching Socks
- Several pairs of socks of different sizes or with different designs (optional)
- Clothesline (*Extend the Experience*)

Number 2 Clap and Clap
- Paper bag
- Construction paper or card stock
- Playing cards ace through nine (optional)

Number 3 Equal Groups
- Resealable plastic bag
- Six paper cups for each pair
- Eighteen beans (or objects of similar size) for each pair

Number 4 Penny Towers
- Twenty pennies for each pair
- Resealable plastic bag for each pair
- Paper cup for each pair

Number 5 Number Drop
- Five cubes or objects of similar size for each pair

Number 6 Make Five
- Six paper cups or other small opaque containers for each pair
- Fifteen beans or other small objects for each pair

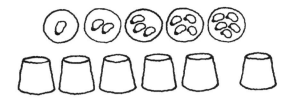

- Construction paper (*Extend the Experience*)
- Five pattern blocks, tiles, or cubes of different colors (*Extend the Experience*)

Measurement 1 Shorter Than a Straw
- Straw for each pair
- Sticky note for each pair

Measurement 2 Stepping Out
- Sticky note for each pair

Geometry 1 Triangle Fun
- Envelopes

Geometry 2 Triangle Puzzles
- Envelopes
- Tangrams (*Extend the Experience*)

Geometry 3 Fold a Square
- Eight-inch by eight-inch paper squares
- Nine-inch by nine-inch sheets of construction paper or tag board

Literature Links
Number
Crews, Donald. *Ten Black Dots* (New York: Scholastic Inc. , 1986)

Guettier, Bénédicte. *The Father Who Had 10 Children* (New York: Dial Books for Young Readers, 1999)

Murphy, Stuart J. *A Pair of Socks* (New York: HarperTrophy, 1996)

Spanish

Bang, Molly. *Diez, Nueve, Ocho* (New York: William Morrow & Company, Inc., 1997)

Walsh, Ellen Stoll. *Cuenta ratones* (Mexico: Fondo De Cultura Económica, S.A. de C.V., 1992)

Measurement
Nathan, Cheryl and McCourt , Lisa. *The Long and Short of It* (New Jersey: Bridgewater Paperback/Troll, 1999)

Myller, Rolf. *How Big Is a Foot?* (New York: Dell Publishing, 1991)

Lionni, Leo. *Inch by Inch* (New York: Scholastic Inc., 1995)

Spanish

Lionni, Leo. *Pulgada a Pulgada* (New York: Scholastic Inc., 1995)

Geometry
Blackstone, Stella. *Bear in a Square* (Bristol: Barefoot Books, 1998)

Dodds, Dayle Ann. *The Shape of Things* (Boston: Candlewick Press, 1996)

Falwell, Cathryn. *Shape Space* (New York: Clarion Books, 1992)

Spanish

Bourgoing , Pascale de and Camil, Colette. *¿Dónde está el triángulo?* (La Galera, 1997)

Hill, Eric. *Spot's Big Book of Colors, Shapes, and Numbers El libro grande de Spot colores, formas y números* (New York: Ventura Publishing Ltd., 1994)

Introducing MATHLINKS to Families

Communicating with families about **MathLinks** will increase their participation and help them understand how to support their children's learning at home. Parents want to know what to expect and what you expect. To help you communicate this, **MathLinks** has included four family letters. The **Introductory Family Letter**, found on p. 11, introduces **MathLinks**, the importance of the activities to the child's mathematical and social development, and the role of the home partner. This letter also suggests a few materials that children and their home partners could collect to have available for the activities. You might want to send this letter home at the beginning of the year.

The other three letters—**Number Activities Family Letter**, p. 13, **Measurement Activities Family Letter**, p. 15, and **Geometry Activities Family Letter**, p. 17—each introduces one of the three sets of activities and includes ideas for additional activities that families can do together and books to read together. The first **MathLinks** activity in each set suggests sending home the family letter for that set with the **At Home** activity.

Other methods are successful for communicating with families. At the beginning of the year, introduce **MathLinks** at Orientation Night or Back-to-School Night. Conduct a **MathLinks** Night to introduce families to the program and the **At Home** activities. Talk about **MathLinks** during parent conferences. Include a **MathLinks** column or **MathLinks** tips section in your class newsletter where you discuss the activities to be sent home that week or month and provide a calendar that indicates when they are due back to school.

Key Ideas for Families

Regardless of how you introduce **MathLinks** to families, here are some important ideas to share with them.

- The **MathLinks** activities give your child more practice with the mathematical concepts we are learning in the classroom.

- The home partner is a learning partner. This means doing the activity with your child. (Note: Parents may have more experience explaining a home assignment and having the child do it by herself or checking the child's work after she has completed a home assignment. Parents may need your help to understand the interactive nature of the home partner role.)

- Conversation is important for your child's learning. Talk with your child as you do the activities. The "talk about" questions suggested in the activity will help you.

- Children need help learning to be responsible. Talk with your child about ways he can remember his responsibilities. The final step in the **At Home** activity suggests things to discuss to help your child *Get Ready for School*.

- The activities need to be returned on time, as the information you and your child write on the **At Home** activity will be used for a class activity.

- You and your child may want to put together a **MathLinks** materials box for the activities with pencils, paper, an eraser, crayons or markers, scissors, tape or a stapler, and beans or some other item to count.

- Keep it simple and fun!

Welcome to MathLinks!

Dear Family,

Once or twice a month your child will bring home an enjoyable fifteen- to twenty-minute **MathLinks At Home** activity. Please work as a partner with your child to collect information, find shapes, measure objects, and play math games.

These **At Home** activities will help your child develop important math skills such as counting, adding, measuring, and recognizing shapes. Your child also will learn to take responsibility for doing the work on time and for taking the **At Home** activity home and back to school.

To make **MathLinks** an enjoyable and successful learning experience, please:

- help your child find a good time and place to work with you.
- help your child find someone else to work with as a home partner when you are not available.
- help your child gather the needed materials for the activities: paper, a pencil, crayons or markers, scissors, and a collection of small objects such as buttons, beans, and pennies. Together, put them in a container and decide on a place to keep them.
- read each **MathLinks At Home** activity with your child before you begin the activity.

Have fun with these activities!

¡Bienvenida a MathLinks!

Estimada familia:

Una o dos veces al mes, su niño traerá a casa una amena actividad **En casa** Mathlinks de quince a veinte minutos de duración. Por favor, trabaje como compañero de su niño para reunir información, buscar figuras, medir objetos y jugar a juegos de matemáticas.

Estas actividades **En casa** ayudarán a su niño a desarrollar importantes destrezas de matemáticas tales como contar, sumar, medir y reconocer figuras. Su niño también aprenderá a responsabilizarse de hacer el trabajo a tiempo y de llevar a casa y traer de vuelta a la escuela la actividad **En casa**.

Para hacer que las actividades de **MathLinks** sean una experiencia de aprendizaje amena y exitosa, por favor:

- ayude a su niño a encontrar un buen lugar y momento para trabajar con usted.
- ayude a su niño a encontrar a alguien más con quien trabajar como compañero en casa cuando usted no esté disponible.
- ayude a su niño a reunir los materiales necesarios para las actividades: papel, un lápiz, creyones o marcadores, tijeras y una colección de objetos pequeños como botones, frijoles y centavos. Juntos, pónganlos en un recipiente y decidan en qué lugar guardarlos.
- lea con su niño cada actividad **En casa** de **MathLinks** antes de empezar la actividad.

¡Tienen mucho gusto con estas actividades!

Learning About Numbers

Dear Family,

Our class is learning about numbers. The attached **MathLinks** activity is the first in a set of six activities that will help your child learn more about numbers at home.

Children learn more when they have a partner to work with and to talk with about their thinking. For these activities, please be your child's home partner. When you cannot be the home partner, please help your child find someone else—an older brother or sister, a grandparent, an aunt or uncle, or a neighbor.

Math Is Everywhere

We use numbers every day of our lives. Here are some simple ideas for helping your child learn more about numbers.

- Point to a group of two, three, or four objects such as rocks, leaves, or apples. Ask your child to tell you the number of objects without counting. Count them together to check.

- Talk with your child about the numbers you use during the day. Think and count aloud when you use numbers: *I need four cups of flour . . . one, two, three, four. I need six nails to build this shelf . . . two, four, six.*

- Make simple math problems about things that happen in your lives. *There are three place mats on the table. If I put out two more, how many place mats will there be?*

- Look for chances to compare things. Ask questions such as: *Are there more children on the swings or on the slides? We have four chairs and three children. Do we have enough chairs?*

At the Library

To help your child learn more about numbers, you may want to read some popular children's counting books together. Try these:

- *Feast for Ten* by Cathryn Falwell (Clarion Books, 1993).

- *Moja Means One* by Muriel Feelings (Dial Books for Young Readers, 1976).

- *Ten, Nine, Eight* by Molly Bang (Mulberry Books, 1983).

The librarian can suggest more books about numbers for you and your child to read and discuss.

Aprender acerca de los números

Estimada familia:

Nuestra clase está aprendiendo acerca de los números. La actividad de **MathLinks** incluida es la primera de seis actividades que ayudarán a su niño a aprender en casa más sobre los números.

Los niños aprenden más cuando tienen un compañero con el que pueden trabajar y hablar sobre lo que piensan. Para estas actividades, por favor sea el compañero en casa de su niño. Cuando usted no puede ser el compañero en casa, por favor ayude a su niño a buscar a alguien más–un hermano o hermana mayor, un abuelo, una tía o un tío, o un vecino.

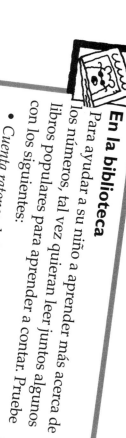

En la biblioteca

Para ayudar a su niño a aprender más acerca de los números, tal vez quieran leer juntos algunos libros populares para aprender a contar. Pruebe con los siguientes:

- *Cuenta ratones de Ellen Stoll Walsh* (Fondo de Cultura Económica, S.A. de C.V., 1992).
- *Diez, Nueve, Ocho de Molly Bang* (William Morrow & Company, Inc., 1997).

El bibliotecario puede aconsejarle otros libros sobre números para que usted y su niño los lean y comenten.

Las matemáticas están en todas partes

Usamos números todos los días. Aquí tiene algunas ideas sencillas para ayudar a su niño a aprender más sobre los números.

- Señale un grupo de dos, tres o cuatro objetos, como piedras, hojas o manzanas. Pida a su niño que le diga el número de objetos que hay sin contarlos. Cuéntenlos juntos para comprobar.

- Hable con su niño sobre los números que usan durante el día. Piense y cuente en voz alta cuando use los números: *Necesito seis tazas de harina...una, dos, tres, cuatro. Necesito seis clavos para construir este estante...dos, cuatro, seis.*

- Haga problemas sencillos de matemáticas sobre cosas que pasan en sus vidas. *Hay tres individuales sobre la mesa. Si pongo dos más, ¿cuántos habrá?*

- Busque oportunidades para comparar cosas. Haga preguntas como éstas: *¿Hay más niños en los columpios o en los toboganes? Tenemos cuatro sillas y tres niños. ¿Tenemos suficientes sillas?*

Learning About Measurement

Dear Family,

Our class is learning about measurement. The attached MathLinks activity is the first in a set of activities that will help your child learn more at home about measurement.

Children learn more when they have a partner to work with and talk with about their thinking. For these activities, please be your child's home partner. When you cannot be your child's home partner, please help your child find someone else—an older brother or sister, a grandparent, an aunt or uncle, or a neighbor.

Math Is Everywhere

Here are some ideas for helping your child learn more about measurement.

- Compare two things, such as a banana and an orange, and discuss which is lighter or heavier, shorter or longer, shorter or taller, wider or thinner.

- Use small objects, such as paper clips or pennies, to measure the length of things such as forks, pencils, leaves, or boxes.

- Talk about things people measure at home or in the neighborhood, such as wood to build a fence or fabric to make curtains, and how they measure them.

At the Library

To help your child learn more about measurement, read some popular children's books together. Try these:

- *How Big Is a Foot?* by Rolf Myller (Dell Publishing, 1991),

- *Inch by Inch* by Leo Lionni (Scholastic Inc., 1995).

- *The Long and Short of It* by Cheryl Nathan and Lisa McCourt (BridgeWater Paperback/Troll, 1999).

The librarian can suggest more books about measurement for you and your child to read and discuss.

Aprender acerca de las medidas

Estimada familia:

Nuestra clase está aprendiendo acerca de las medidas. La actividad de **MathLinks** incluida es la primera de un grupo de actividades que ayudarán a su niño a aprender más en casa sobre las medidas.

Los niños aprenden más cuando tienen un compañero con el que pueden trabajar y hablar sobre lo que piensan. Para estas actividades, por favor sea el compañero en casa de su niño. Cuando usted no puede ser el compañero en casa de su niño, por favor ayúdele a buscar a alguien más–un hermano o hermana mayor, un abuelo, una tía o tío o un vecino.

En la biblioteca

Para que su niño aprenda más acerca de las medidas, lean juntos algunos libros populares de niños. Cuatro de ellos son:

- *How Big Is a Foot?* de Rolf Myller (Dell Publishing, 1991),
- *Inch by Inch* de Leo Lionni (Scholastic Inc., 1995).
- *The Long and Short of It* de Cheryl Nathan y Lisa McCourt (BridgeWater PaperBack/Troll, 1999),
- *La semilla de zanahoria* de Ruth Krauss (Scholastic Inc. 1978).

El bibliotecario puede aconsejarle más libros sobre medidas para que usted y su niño los lean y los comenten.

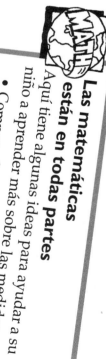

Las matemáticas están en todas partes

Aquí tiene algunas ideas para ayudar a su niño a aprender más sobre las medidas.

- Compare dos cosas, como una naranja y una banana y comenten cuál es más liviana o más pesada, más larga o más corta, más baja o más alta, más ancha o más delgada.

- Use objetos pequeños, como sujetapapeles o centavos, para medir la longitud de cosas como tenedores, lápices, hojas o cajas.

- Hable sobre cosas que mide la gente en casa o en el vecindario, como la madera para construir una cerca o la tela para hacer cortinas, y cómo las miden.

Learning About Geometry

Dear Family,

Our class is learning about geometry. The attached **MathLinks** activity is the first in a set of activities that will help your child learn more about geometry.

Children learn more when they have a partner to work with and to talk with about their thinking. For these activities, please be your child's home partner. When you cannot be the home partner, please help your child find someone else—an older brother or sister, a grandparent, an aunt or an uncle, or a neighbor.

Math Is Everywhere

Here are some ideas for helping your child learn more about geometry.

- Look for shapes such as triangles, rectangles, squares, and circles on fabric, wallpaper, and rugs.
- Take a walk and look for shapes on buildings, at the playground, or in store windows.
- Together draw designs or imaginary creatures using triangles, rectangles, squares, and circles.

At the Library

To help your child learn more about geometry, read some children's books together. Try these:

- *The Shape of Things* by Dayle Ann Dodds (Candlewick Press, 1996).
- *Shape Space* by Cathryn Falwell (Clarion Books, 1992).
- *Bear in a Square* by Stella Blackstone (Barefoot Books, 1998).

The librarian can suggest more books about geometry for you and your child to read and discuss.

Aprender acerca de la geometría

Estimada familia:

Nuestra clase está aprendiendo acerca de la geometría. La actividad de **MathLinks** incluida es la primera de un grupo actividades que ayudarán a su niño a aprender en casa más sobre geometría.

Los niños aprenden más cuando tienen un compañero con quien trabajar y hablar sobre lo que piensan. Para estas actividades, por favor sea el compañero en casa de su niño. Cuando usted no puede ser el compañero en casa, por favor ayude a su niño a encontrar a alguien más–un hermano o hermana mayor, un abuelo, una tía o un tío o un vecino.

Las matemáticas están en todas partes

Aquí tiene algunas ideas para ayudar a su niño a aprender más sobre geometría.

- Busquen figuras geométricas, tales como triángulos, rectángulos, círculos en telas, papel de empapelar y alfombras.

- Vayan de paseo y busquen figuras geométricas en edificios, en el patio de recreo o en las vitrinas de las tiendas.

- Dibujen juntos diseños o criaturas imaginarias usando triángulos, rectángulos, cuadrados y círculos.

En la biblioteca

Para ayudar a su niño a aprender más algunos libros para niños. Cuatro libros populares sobre geometría, lean juntos son:

- *The Shape of Things* de Dayle Ann Dodds
- *Shape Space* de Cathryn Falwell (Candlewick Press, 1996).
- *Bear in a Square* de Stella Blackstone (Clarion Books, 1992).
- *Spot's Big Book of Colors, Shapes and Numbers/ El libro grande de Spot, colores, formas y números* de Eric Hill (Ventura Publishing Ltd., 1994).

El bibliotecario puede sugerirle más libros sobre geometría para que usted y su niño los lean y comenten.

Learning to Work Together

In addition to supporting children's mathematical development, **MathLinks** strives to promote their ability to work with others, communicate their thinking, and be responsible learners. **MathLinks** provides many opportunities for children to work with others—with school partners for the **At School** and the **Back at School** activities and home partners for the **At Home** activity. Most kindergarten children are ready to learn to work with a partner. **MathLinks** helps them develop important initial group skills such as taking turns, sharing the work and materials, and listening to a partner.

The MathLinks Approach

The **MathLinks** approach to cooperative work includes elements common to most cooperative learning methods: children work in heterogeneous groups as they pursue a common goal; they are actively involved in their learning; and they have ongoing opportunities to share ideas, discuss their thinking, and listen to the thinking of others.

The **MathLinks** approach differs from other cooperative learning methods in several respects, particularly in its focus on children's social development. In addition to basic group skills, **MathLinks**

fosters children's ability to be responsible and fair and to make effective decisions. Another difference is that **MathLinks** does not specify roles for cooperative work. Instead, children make decisions about how they will divide the work and how they will record and report their findings. Children talk about how they make these decisions and whether the process is fair. Such discussion helps them learn from and build on their experiences.

Beginning Cooperative Work

Learning to cooperate is a developmental process and can be difficult for children, particularly in the beginning of the year. Start by helping children develop a sense of identity and community as a class. Activities such as developing a class name, logo, or handshake are important to creating an "our classroom" feeling.

Helping children develop the desire and skills to support each other and cooperate is an ongoing process. At the beginning of the year, have children set norms for how they want to work together. Refer to these norms each day and revise them as needed. Throughout the year, continue to develop the spirit of community in your classroom. This is particularly important after a long vacation, if you have been out of the classroom for a few days, after illness has kept many children home, or when new children arrive in your class. Sources for class-building activities include Developmental Studies Center's *Among Friends*; Gibbs's *Tribes: A New Way of Learning and Being Together*, Hill and Hill's *The Collaborative Classroom*; Moorman and Dishon's *Our Classroom: We Can*

Learn Together; and Rhoades and McCabe's *The Nurturing Classroom.* See Additional Reading, pp. 209–211.

The physical set-up of your classroom is an important factor in creating an environment that supports cooperation. The arrangement should allow partners easy access to each other and to materials. Sharing a small table or sitting at adjacent desks is a good arrangement for a pair. It also is important to have space in the classroom where the entire class can meet (in a circle, if possible) for whole-class discussions.

Forming Pairs

When you are ready to begin cooperative work, randomly assign children as partners. This gives children several positive messages: there is no hidden plan behind how you grouped them (such as choosing partners based on achievement); every child is considered a valuable partner; and everyone is expected to learn to work with everyone else. Random assignment also results in heterogeneous pairs, which is important for cooperative work (even though it is inevitable the pairs might be homogenous in some way—for example, both girls). Several suggestions for randomly pairing your children are listed below; other suggestions can be found in Johnson, Johnson, and Holubec's *The New Circles of Learning,* listed in Additional Reading, pp. 209–211.

- Have children find someone in the room who likes the same dessert or who has a different favorite color.

- Cut magazine pictures in half. Have children pick a half and then find the person with the other half of the picture.

- For half of the class, make chains of different lengths with plastic links. For the other half of the class, make index cards each with the length of one of the chains written as a numeral on it. Randomly distribute the cards and chains to children and have them find a partner with a card that matches their chain or chain that matches their card.

- Cut strings in different lengths, two per length. Have children pick a string and then find the person with the string of the same length.

Sharing in Pairs

The **MathLinks** activities suggest several easily implemented cooperative strategies that help children talk about their thinking with others. Information about these strategies is listed below. For more strategies, see Developmental Studies Center's *Blueprints for a Cooperative Classroom* and Kagan's *Cooperative Learning,* both listed in Additional Reading, pp. 209–211.

Turn to Your Partner

Turn to Your Partner is a very informal and easy strategy: When you ask a question or pose a problem, have children turn to their partner or to someone sitting next to them to discuss it. If you are trying cooperative strategies for the first time, this is a good beginning strategy. *Turn to Your Partner* is suggested in the Number

Activities—"Equal Groups," "Penny Towers," and "Make Five"; the Measurement Activity—"Shorter Than a Straw"; and the Geometry Activities—"Triangle Puzzles" and "Fold a Square."

Think, Pair, Share

The *Think, Pair, Share* strategy is useful for more complex questions or for questions that require analysis, such as about data that has been collected. It gives children some time to think before offering their ideas. To use this strategy, ask a question or pose a problem and allow some time for individual reflection. Then ask children to discuss their thoughts with their partner. Finally, have pairs share their thinking with another pair or with the class. This strategy is suggested in the Number Activities—"Equal Groups," "Number Drop," and "Make Five"; the Measurement Activities—"Stepping Out" and "Handy Measurements"; and the Geometry Activity—"Triangle Fun."

Pair Q and A

Pair Q and A helps children learn to ask each other questions and to listen to their partners. This strategy gets more sophisticated as children get older and are more able to converse with each other. For kindergarten children, model how to ask a question and then have partners take turns asking each other and answering the question. Afterwards, have a few pairs share their thinking with the class. In the beginning of the year, ask children to share their own thinking; later, as they become more capable, ask children to report their partner's thinking. This strategy is suggested in the Number Activities—"Matching Socks," "Clap and Clap," and "Penny Towers"; the Measurement Activity—"Stepping Out"; and the Geometry Activity—"Fold a Square."

Often the **MathLinks** activities suggest that children talk about something or share their work in pairs or with the class without suggesting a specific strategy. Choose any of the strategies above or one of the following two strategies not suggested in the activities.

Tea Party

Tea Party gives pairs a chance to move around as they share their thinking with several other pairs. You begin by having pairs circulate around the classroom. When you call "Tea Party," the pairs stop and turn to the nearest pair to form a "tea party" of four. You then ask a question or give a topic for the "tea parties" to discuss. At your signal, the tea party pairs say good-bye to each other and begin walking around the room until you again call "Tea Party."

This strategy takes some practice. Children first need to practice walking around the room with their partner. They also need to practice finding and greeting another pair when you call "Tea Party." Once your class is able to do this, begin with an easy topic for the tea party, such as having them tell each other about their favorite food, color, or what they like to do after school; or showing each other and explaining pictures that they have drawn. When children are ready for an academic tea party topic, you might ask pairs to tell each other what they know about a shape or ask them to talk about a mathematical problem.

Strolling

Strolling is literally that: children display their work on their desks or tables, then walk around the room to view others' work. Children can stroll individually, in pairs, or in groups, and can talk about what they see as they stroll or after they stroll.

Your Role

In addition to helping prepare children to work together and setting an environment that encourages cooperation, your role includes planning, modeling, and facilitating the cooperative work, and helping children reflect on the mathematics and their group interaction.

Planning

Before a **MathLinks** activity, decide how you will help children think about how they work together. You may decide to emphasize cooperative skills with which your children are having difficulties or you may decide to discuss a specific social skill suggested in the activity.

In either case, you need to plan when and how to have these discussions. You may want to ask children at the beginning of an activity to discuss a skill that you've chosen; for example, they might discuss the strategies they've learned about how to share the work with a partner. Or, after children understand the activity, you might ask them to discuss how they might share the work of the activity. Another option is during the activity to ask pairs how they are sharing the work and whether that method is fair to both partners. Finally, you might have a class discussion at the end of the activity about ways children discovered

to share the work and why those ways worked for them.

Consider two other options—instead of determining the cooperative skills ahead of time, discuss issues as they arise or ask children which skills they think they'll need or want to work on. Vary your approach to keep it fresh and useful for children.

Modeling

MathLinks activities suggest that you model the activity for the class, either with a child as your partner or by asking a pair to demonstrate. (See **At School** p. 4.) Including children in the modeling is more powerful than just demonstrating the activity yourself as it provides an example of how partners can work together and some of the problems they may experience. Such concrete examples help children discover ways to work responsibly during the activity and what they can do when problems arise.

Facilitating Pair Work

As children begin to work, observe each pair to ensure that they understand the activity and face no problems that they cannot solve themselves. Then focus on a few pairs and observe each long enough to understand what's happening. This will give you information about children's ability to work together, their engagement in the activity, and their mathematical

understanding. You also will generate ideas for questions to ask the pair or to discuss with the class. (Questions are suggested in each **MathLinks** activity as well.)

At times during pair work you may decide to intervene in order to refocus the pair, help them see a problem from another perspective, ask questions that extend their mathematical and social learning, or assess their understanding. When intervening, look for a natural pause in the action so as to avoid interrupting the flow of the pair's work. When partners are having interpersonal difficulties, give them time to resolve the situation themselves. Avoid solving the problem for them or giving lengthy explanations; rather, ask questions that help them find their own way through the difficulty.

Facilitating Reflection

MathLinks uses such strategies as pair discussion, drawing and writing, and whole-class discussion to promote reflection. In most instances, the activities suggest that children talk about their thinking first with a partner, and then as a class. Sharing with a partner first allows all children to discuss their thinking and is often more comfortable for them.

At first, young children may have difficulty explaining their thinking, but their ability to express themselves will improve with practice and with the opportunity to hear other children's explanations. To help children be more willing to risk sharing their thinking, accept whatever the child is able to express and make gentle use of probing questions. Encourage children to be respectful as they ask each other questions about their strategies and their thinking.

Your use of probing, open-ended questions is critical to helping children develop their mathematical understanding and ability to work together and take responsibility. Throughout each **MathLinks** activity questions are suggested to help children discuss and examine their thinking and rely on their own authority. Ask questions that require progressively more thought or understanding. Encourage children to consider such important issues as

- what they have learned,

- how their learning relates to their previous experience or daily life,

- what it means to be responsible, and

- how their behavior affects their partners' and their own learning.

Supporting the NCTM Standards with MATHLINKS

Principles and Standards **Matrix**

MathLinks activities are designed to support the *Principles and Standards for School Mathematics* developed by the National Council of Teachers of Mathematics (NCTM). The following matrix correlates the kindergarten **MathLinks** activities with the Pre-K-2 Number, Measurement, and Geometry Standards.

Number

NCTM Expectations	Matching Socks	Clap and Clap	Equal Groups	Penny Towers	Number Drop	Make Five
Count with understanding and recognize "how many" in sets of objects	X	X	X	X	X	X
Develop a sense of whole numbers and represent and use them in flexible ways, including relating, composing, and decomposing numbers	X	X	X	X	X	X
Connect number words and numerals to the quantities they represent, using various physical models and representations		X			X	X
Understand the effects of adding and subtracting whole numbers					X	X
Develop and use strategies for whole-number computations, with a focus on addition and subtraction					X	X
Use a variety of methods and tools to compute, including objects, mental computation, estimation, paper and pencil, and calculators					X	X

MathLinks *Principles and Standards* Matrix (continued)

Measurement

NCTM Expectations	Shorter Than a Straw	Stepping Out	Handy Measurements
Recognize the attributes of length, volume, weight, area, and time	X	X	X
Compare and order objects according to these attributes	X		
Understand how to measure using nonstandard and standard units		X	X
Use repetition of a single unit to measure something larger than the unit, for instance, measuring the length of a room with a single meter stick		X	X
Use tools to measure	X	X	X

Geometry

NCTM Expectations	Triangle Fun	Triangle Puzzles	Fold a Square
Recognize, name, build, draw, compare, and sort two-and three-dimensional shapes	X	X	X
Describe attributes and parts of two-and-three dimensional shapes	X	X	X
Investigate and predict the results of putting together and taking apart two- and three-dimensional shapes	X	X	X
Recognize geometric shapes and structures in the environment and specify their location	X	X	X

Using MATHLINKS with Reform Curricula

MathLinks is aligned with several curricula: *Everyday Mathematics, Investigations in Number, Data and Space, Math Trailblazers, Number Power* and *Mathland*. The following matrices suggest a correlation with each program. A key to help you understand the correlation follows each matrix.

Number Matrix

Number Activities	Everyday Mathematics	Investigations in Number, Data, and Space	Mathland	Math Trailblazers	Number Power
Matching Socks	After "Attribute Blocks," p. 37 Before "What's My Rule, Fishing," p. 99	Before <u>Mathematical Thinking in Kindergarten</u>, Investigation 2, "Counting Jar," pp. 24–31 *Before <u>Collecting, Counting, and Measuring</u>, Investigation 1, "Counting Books," pp. 4–9*	Before <u>Let's Count</u>, "Teddy Bears One to Ten," pp. 140–147 *Before <u>Let's Count</u>, "At the Zoo," pp. 166–173*	Before <u>Number Sense</u>, "Our Number Books," pp. 115–116 *After <u>Number Sense</u>, "What Can We Count?" pp. 110–112*	With <u>Set 1, Exploring Numbers</u>, "Domino, Domino! 1," pp. 15–24 *After <u>Set 1, Exploring Numbers</u>, "Chickety, Chickety, Chop," pp. 43–45*
Clap and Clap	After "Listen and Count," p. 21 Before "Give the Next Number," p. 33	Before <u>Collecting, Counting, and Measuring</u>, Investigation 2, "Taking Inventory," pp. 23–29 *Before <u>Collecting, Counting, and Measuring</u>, Investigation 6, "Six Tiles," pp. 80–85*	After <u>Let's Count</u>, "Teddy Bears One to Ten," pp. 140–147 *After <u>Beginning Numbers</u>, "Number Shapes," pp. 82–89*	After <u>Number Sense</u>, "Connecting Objects to Symbols," pp. 112–113 *Before <u>Number Sense</u>, "No Ones! Game," p. 119*	Before <u>Set 1, Exploring Numbers</u>, "Handy-Dandy," pp. 53–55 *With <u>Set 2, Exploring Numbers and Operations</u>, "Elephants Play," pp. 103–105*
Equal Groups	After "Finger Counting," p. 36 Before "Concentration With Number Cards and Dominoes," p. 89	With <u>Collecting, Counting, and Measuring</u>, Investigation 4, "Letters in Our Names," pp. 54–59 *With <u>Collecting, Counting, and Measuring</u>, Investigation 5, "Least to Most," pp. 68–71*	Before <u>Let's Count</u>, "Bears in Chairs," pp. 156–163 *After <u>Let's Count</u>, "Teddy Bears One to Ten," pp. 142–147*	Before <u>Number Sense</u>, "More Than, Less Than, the Same as Flash," p. 132 *Before <u>Number Sense</u>, "Domino Sort," pp. 137–139*	Before <u>Set 2, Exploring Numbers and Operations</u>, "Match It!" pp. 123–138 *With <u>Set 1, Exploring Numbers</u>, "Domino, Domino! 2," pp. 25–42*

Number Martix

Number Activities	Everyday Mathematics	Investigations in Number, Data, and Space	Mathland	Math Trailblazers	Number Power
Penny Towers	*After "Teen Partner Game (10–20)," p. 82* *Before "Listen and Do (10–20)," p. 116*	**Before <u>Collecting, Counting, and Measuring</u>, Investigation 2, "Taking Inventory," pp. 24–29** *Before <u>Collecting, Counting, and Measuring</u>, Investigation 1, "Counting Books," pp. 4–9*	**Before <u>Numbers Big and Small</u>, "Big Number Count," pp. 262–269** *Before <u>Let's Count</u>, "Factory Orders," pp. 148–155*	**Before <u>Number Sense</u>, "Cube Towers," p. 133** *Or when children are practicing how to count twenty objects accurately and tell which of two numbers is more or less*	With <u>Set 1, Exploring Numbers</u>, "Let's Go Fishing," pp. 11–13
Number Drop	*After "Introduction to Collections of Number Names," p. 210* **Before "Bead String Name Collections," p. 231**	**With <u>How Many in All?</u>, Investigation 4, "Blue and Red Crayons," pp. 76–81** *With <u>How Many in All?</u>, Investigation 2, "Six Tiles in All," pp. 30–37*	**Before <u>Numbers Big and Small</u>, "Box Car Builders," pp. 254–261**	**With <u>Number Sense</u>, "Five on the Mat," p. 130** *Before <u>Number Sense</u>, "Benny's Pennies," pp. 124–125*	**Before Set 2, <u>Exploring Numbers and Operations</u>, "More Dominoes," pp. 63–93** *Before Set 2, <u>Exploring Numbers and Operations</u>, "Domino Booklet," pp. 95–102*
Make Five	**After "Which Operation Do I Need?" p. 209** *Before "Craft Stick Name Collections," p. 232*	**With <u>How Many in All?</u>, Investigation 2, "Six Tiles in All," pp. 30–37** *With <u>How Many in All?</u>, Investigation 4, "Blue and Red Crayons," pp. 76–81*	**Before <u>Numbers Big and Small</u>, "Box Car Builders," pp. 254–261**	**Before <u>Number Sense</u>, "Rings on My Fingers," pp. 126–127** *Before <u>Number Sense</u>, "Five Little Monkeys," pp. 128–129*	**Before Set 2, <u>Exploring Numbers and Operations</u>, "Elephant Stories," pp. 107–109** *Before <u>Set 3, Exploring Computation and Problem Solving</u>, "Here a Piggie," pp. 149–166*

- **Bold type** indicates where an activity fits best.
- *Italics* indicates a secondary fit.
- "Before" indicates that the concepts and skills in a **MathLinks** activity will help prepare children for the lesson.
- "With" indicates that the conceptual understandings in **MathLinks** are similar to those in the lesson. The **MathLinks** activity may be used at any point before, during, or after the lesson.
- "After" indicates that a **MathLinks** activity either extends the concepts explored in the lesson or requires an understanding of the concepts developed in that lesson.

Measurement Matrix

Measurement Activities	Everyday Mathematics	Investigations in Number, Data, and Space	Mathland	Math Trailblazers
Shorter Than a Straw	After "Comparing Lengths," p. 43 Before "Arranging Items By Length," p. 135	With <u>Collecting, Counting, and Measuring,</u> Investigation 3, "Measurement Towers," pp. 38–41	Before <u>Long and Short,</u> "Strings and Things," pp. 216–223	Before <u>Measurement,</u> "Length Comparisons," p. 205 *Before <u>Measurement,</u> "As Tall As a ___?" pp. 200–202*
Stepping Out	With "Measuring with Children's Feet," p. 136	After <u>How Many in All?,</u> Investigation 1, "Counting and Measuring," pp. 4–11	After <u>Long and Short,</u> "Bring a Buddy," pp. 224–231	Before <u>Measurement,</u> "If the Shoe Fits," p. 207 *Before <u>Measurement,</u> "Teddy Bear Lineup," pp. 209–210*
Handy Measurements	Before "Marking Off Lengths," p. 148	After <u>How Many in All?,</u> Investigation 1, "Counting and Measuring," pp. 4–11	After <u>Long and Short,</u> "Bring a Buddy," pp. 224–231	Before <u>Measurement,</u> "Measuring with Shoes," pp. 207–208 *With <u>Measurement,</u> "Jumpers!" p. 211*

- **Bold type** indicates where an activity fits best.
- *Italics* indicates a secondary fit.
- "Before" indicates that the concepts and skills in a **MathLinks** activity will help prepare children for the lesson.
- "With" indicates that the conceptual understandings in **MathLinks** are similar to those in the lesson. The **MathLinks** activity may be used at any point before, during, or after the lesson.
- "After" indicates that a **MathLinks** activity either extends the concepts explored in the lesson or requires an understanding of the concepts developed in that lesson.

Geometry Matrix

Geometry Activities	Everyday Mathematics	Investigations in Number, Data, and Space	Mathland	Math Trailblazers
Triangle Fun	*After "Printing Shapes," pg 195* **Before "Comparing Shapes," p. 218–219**	**After <u>Making Shapes and Building Blocks,</u> Investigation 1, "Looking at 2-D Shapes," pp. 4–11**	**Before <u>Shapes,</u> "Puzzles and Pieces," pp. 186–193**	**With <u>Geometry,</u> "Looking for Shapes," p. 181** *With <u>Geometry,</u> "Mystery Shape," p. 183*
Triangle Puzzles	*With "I Spy," p. 220*	**Before <u>Making Shapes and Building Blocks,</u> Investigation 2, "Introducing the Shapes Software," pp. 28–30** *With <u>Making Shapes and Building Blocks,</u> Investigation 4, "Clay Shapes," pp. 62–67*	**With <u>Shapes,</u> "Puzzles and Pieces," pp. 186–193**	**Before <u>Geometry,</u> "Shapes on the Geoboard," p. 186** *After <u>Geometry,</u> "Making a Pattern Block Clown," p. 184*
Fold a Square	**With "Paper Folding Geom-etry," p. 105**	**With <u>Making Shapes and Building Blocks,</u> Investigation 4, "Clay Shapes," pp. 62–67** *Before <u>Making Shapes and Building Blocks,</u> Investigation 5, "A Close Look at Geoblocks," pp. 84–87*	**With <u>Shapes,</u> "Puzzles and Pieces," pp. 186–193**	**After <u>Geometry,</u> "Shapes on a Geoboard," pp. 186–187** *After <u>Geometry,</u> "Making a Pattern Block Clown," p. 184*

- **Bold type** indicates where an activity fits best.
- *Italics* indicates a secondary fit.
- "Before" indicates that the concepts and skills in a **MathLinks** activity will help prepare children for the lesson.
- "With" indicates that the conceptual understandings in **MathLinks** are similar to those in the lesson. The **MathLinks** activity may be used at any point before, during, or after the lesson.
- "After" indicates that a **MathLinks** activity either extends the concepts explored in the lesson or requires an understanding of the concepts developed in that lesson.

Number Activities Overview

NUMBER CONCEPTS

A sound understanding of number is indispensable to making sense of the world and is the primary goal of elementary mathematics instruction. For kindergarten, the focus for number instruction is on developing children's counting skills—particularly helping them count with accuracy and meaning—and on developing their understanding of number relationships. The **MathLinks** number activities focus on developing these skills and concepts and help children learn to compare attributes and quantities of objects and explore number combinations for five.

Count with Accuracy and Meaning

Learning to count requires a set of complex, sophisticated skills and concepts.

* *Counting Sequence*
  Child can say the number names by rote, but may not understand their meaning.

* *One-to-one correspondence*
  Child can count by saying a number name for each object in a group with accuracy, first with small groups of objects and gradually counting and keeping track of objects in larger groups.

* *Cardinality*
  Child understands that the last number said when counting a group of objects names the total number in the group.

* *Conservation*
  Child understands that a quantity remains the same no matter how it is arranged.

* *Subitizing*
  Child recognizes small quantities without counting—initially seeing groups of two and three without counting, then seeing four through ten (by recognizing the number either as a whole or as made up of smaller groups).

* *Counting by groups*
  Child can count by group sizes other than one, such as by twos, fives, and tens. This requires that the child can see a group of two, for example, as one group of two and as two individual objects.

All six of the **MathLinks** number activities help children develop counting skills and concepts.

Understand Number Relationships

Understanding number relationships helps children develop flexibility with numbers, central to number sense, and provides them with the foundation necessary for mental computation and mastery of basic mathematical facts.

- *More than, less than, equal to*
  Child understands the meaning of these terms (for example that four is less than five, more than three and equal to half of eight), is able to remove or add one or two objects to a group and, without recounting, identify the new total.

- *Relationships to five and ten*
  Child uses five and ten as referents to think about and compute with other numbers (for example, thinking of eight as three more than five or two less than ten, and using this knowledge as they add and subtract).

- *Relative magnitude*
  Child understands that a number can be small, large, or about the same size depending on the numbers to which it is compared (for example, nine is small compared to sixty-eight, large compared to one, and about the same as ten).

- *Part-part–whole relationships*
  Child can think of a number as both a whole quantity and as being made of smaller quantities or parts (for example, six is the whole quantity of six and is made of smaller parts, such as five and one, three and three, two and two and two).

All six of the **MathLinks** number activities provide opportunities for children to explore number relationships.

Make Comparisons

The ability to make comparisons is fundamental to the development of many number skills and concepts. Comparing the attributes of objects helps children develop the skills to compare numbers and quantities. In the **MathLinks** activity, "Matching Socks," children compare such attributes as size, color, pattern, and design, as they match pairs of socks. In most of the other kindergarten number activities children compare quantities. In "Equal Groups," for example, children compare quantities to determine whether they are equal.

Explore Number Combinations

Developing fluency with basic number combinations is essential for children. Learning that numbers are composed of other numbers (for example, five is made of four and one, or two and three, or five and zero) is key to developing this fluency. In the **MathLinks** activity "Number Drop" children explore ways to make five.

Learning about Number

The following table identifies the specific number concepts developed in each of the activities. A solid bullet (●) identifies the main focus of an activity and an open bullet (○) identifies other concepts developed.

	1. Matching Socks	2. Clap and Clap	3. Equal Groups	4. Penny Towers	5. Number Drop	6. Make Five
Count using one-to-one correspondence	●	●	●	●	○	●
Compare objects by their attributes	●					
Compare quantities	●		●	●	●	
Recognize number in a group without counting			●		●	○
Explore more than/less than/equal to relationships	○		○	○		
Explore number combinations to 5					●	●
Use mathematical language	●	●	●	●	●	●

WORKING TOGETHER

In the **MathLinks** activities, children work with partners at school and at home. The goal is to enhance their mathematical development while at the same time help them learn to work together successfully, communicate effectively, and be responsible learners.

Work with Others

Most kindergarten children are ready to begin to work with a partner. The **MathLinks** number activities help children develop initial group skills such as sharing the work, listening to a partner, helping each other, and making decisions together.

Communicate Thinking

The **MathLinks** activities provide frequent opportunities for children to discuss their thinking with school and home partners and with the class. An important goal is for children to communicate about mathematics and about how they work together. Equally important is for children to exchange points of view. The activities suggest open-ended questions to achieve these goals, including How do you know? Why do you think that is fair? Why do you think that is a good strategy? Do you agree? Does anyone have another opinion? Such exchanges help children learn

to express their ideas and rethink them when they hear the ideas of others. As children play the games in the **MathLinks** number activities, they explain their strategies and consider those of others. In the **Back at School** activities children frequently tell the entire class about their thinking and their experiences with the home activity. In "Matching Socks," for example, children tell the class about the pairs of socks they matched at home and the class uses this information to do some mathematical thinking.

Be Responsible

Helping children learn to be responsible means giving them opportunities to assume responsibility and helping them acquire strategies to do so successfully. Children's understanding of what it means to be responsible and how to be responsible develops over time, with many experiences, and with opportunities to talk about them. **MathLinks** helps children be responsible for

- their learning and behavior in school and at home

- getting the home activities to and from home

- finding a home partner and completing the activities

- at times, teaching something to a home partner

- explaining to others what they did at school and at home.

Learning to Work Together

The following table identifies the social skills focus of each activity. An solid bullet (●) identifies a main focus, and an open bullet (○) identifies other skills children might practice.

	1. Matching Socks	2. Clap and Clap	3. Equal Groups	4. Penny Towers	5. Number Drop	6. Make Five
Share the work	●	○	○	●	○	○
Teach a game to a home partner		●	○	○	○	○
Listen to a partner	○	●	○	○	○	○
Talk in front of the class	●	○	○	○	○	○
Make decisions together		○	●	○	●	○
Help each other	○	○	○	○	○	●

NUMBER ACTIVITIES AT A GLANCE

1. Matching Socks

Each pair makes a pair of matching paper socks, which are then used for a class activity. Children and their home partners count and match real socks and choose one to draw on their **At Home** activity. Back at school, children discuss the **At Home** activity.

2. Clap and Clap

Partners play "Clap and Clap," a game that helps them count to ten. Children and their home partners play the same game and write or draw about one of their games. Back at school, children discuss the **At Home** activity and play "Clap and Clap" as a group.

3. Equal Groups

Pairs play a game in which they cover groups of two, three, and four objects with cups, and then raise two cups at a time to find equal groups. Children and their home partner play the game and record two of their turns. Back at school, children determine the number of dots on a card without counting and use this skill to compare groups of objects recorded on their **At Home** activities.

4. Penny Towers

Pairs play a game in which they build towers of up to twenty pennies, and then count the pennies when they complete the tower or the tower falls. Children and their home partner play the same game and record their results. Back at school, children discuss the towers they built at home.

5. Number Drop

Pairs play a game in which they take turns dropping five cubes onto a circle. For each turn they find the number of cubes that fall inside and outside the circle. Children and their home partner play the game and record their turns. Back at school, children discuss the results of their games and number combinations for five.

6. Make Five

Pairs play a game in which they uncover two groups of beans at a time to find a total of five beans. Children and their home partners play the same game and record the ways they find to make five. Back at school, children discuss combinations for five and play a guessing game using their **At Home** activities.

LITERATURE LINKS
. . . .

A Pair of Socks by Stuart J. Murphy
(Harper Trophy, 1996). This is the story of a striped sock that searches the house for its mate. The striped sock finds many other socks and finally discovers its mate in the dog's basket. Reading this book as an introduction to "Matching Socks" will help children understand the concept of a matching pair of socks before they make and match paper socks.

The Father Who Had 10 Children by Bénédicte Guettier (Dial Books for Young Readers, a division of Penguin Putnam Inc., 1999). This book shows the frantic, busy life of a single father and his ten children. In the morning he cooks ten

breakfasts and helps his children put on ten pairs of underpants, ten t-shirts, ten jeans, twenty socks, and twenty little shoes. He later decides to leave the children with their grandma and sets sail by himself "around the world for 10 days, or maybe even 10 months." After one night alone, he realizes something is missing and comes back to pick up his ten children to join him on his journey. Read this book before playing "Clap and Clap" to spark a conversation about the number ten.

Ten Black Dots by Donald Crews
(Scholastic Inc., 1986). This book presents groups of increasing numbers of dots in different settings, providing children with fun and fanciful opportunities to practice counting objects in groups. Reading this book as an introduction to "Equal Groups" will help children understand the concept of a group.

Cuenta ratones by Ellen Stoll Walsh
(Fondo De Cultura Económica, S.A. de C.V., 1992). In this counting book, a famished snake counts and captures ten mice in a jar. The mice are able to escape their fate by convincing the snake to pursue a "large mouse" across the way. When the snake is otherwise engaged, the mice tip over the jar and count backward from ten as they each escape. This book will help children practice counting forward and backward.

Diez, Nueve, Ocho by Molly Bang
(William Morrow & Company, Inc., 1997). A loving father prepares his daughter for bed with a countdown that starts "10 small toes all washed and warm" and ends "1 big girl all ready for bed." Read this book to help children practice counting backward.

Matching Socks

AT SCHOOL

In pairs, children decorate and cut out a pair of matching socks. The socks are gathered and then distributed randomly. Children find the person with a matching sock. The class discusses the socks.

AT HOME

Children and their home partners gather, match, and count the family's socks. They choose and draw one of the socks.

BACK AT SCHOOL

After discussing the **At Home** activity, children show the class the paper sock each made at home.

Learning About Number

In this activity, children:

- count using one-to-one correspondence
- compare objects by their attributes
- compare quantities.

Learning to Work Together

In this activity, children:

- share the work
- talk in front of the class.

Mathematical Vocabulary

pair	par
match	emparejar
sort	ordenar
count	contar
group	grupo

AT SCHOOL

Get Ready

1. Determine how you will select partners. (See **Forming Pairs,** p. 201.)

2. Prepare materials:

   - A copy of the Number Activities Family Letter, p. 13, for each child (You may want to attach it to the **At Home** activity.)

   - A copy of the **At Home** activity, with the return date written on it, for each child

   - A copy of "Socks Pattern," p. 44, for each pair and two for modeling (If children have not had much experience working with a partner, you may decide to have them work individually. In that case, you will need a copy of "Socks Pattern" for each child and two for modeling.)

   - A pencil for each child and for the teacher

   - Scissors for each pair

   - Several pairs of socks of different sizes or with different designs (optional)

Literature Link
A Pair of Socks by Stuart J. Murphy (Harper Trophy, 1996). Introduce the activity with this book to help children understand the concept of a matching pair of socks. (optional)

Make Connections

1. Select pairs and have partners sit together. Talk about the chores the children do at home and how this helps their family.

2. Discuss helping with the laundry:

   Whole Class in Pairs

   ? **How do you help your family with the laundry?**

   ? **Does anyone help match pairs of socks when the laundry is done? How many socks make one pair?**

   ? **What do you look for when you match socks? How do you know you have found a pair of matching socks?**

Teacher Tip
If you brought socks to class, show them and ask children how they are the same and how they are different. Then use them to demonstrate the idea of matching a pair of socks.

(¿) *¿Cómo ayudan a su familia con la ropa sucia?*

(¿) *¿Ayuda alguien a emparejar los pares de calcetines cuando la ropa está limpia? ¿Cuántos calcetines forman un par?*

(¿) *¿En qué se fijan cuando emparejan calcetines? ¿Cómo saben si un par de calcetines forma una pareja?*

Explain and Model the Activity

1. Show a "Socks Pattern" and explain that pairs will make a matching pair of socks.

2. Choose a volunteer to help you model the activity. On a "Socks Pattern" draw something that can be counted, such as five triangles. Have your partner copy your design on his own "Socks Pattern" so that your socks look the same. Switch roles and have your partner draw a design on his sock for you to copy on yours. Then cut out your socks. As you model, discuss with the class:

> **Activity Directions**
> - One partner draws a design on his sock with things that can be counted.
> - The other partner copies the design on her sock.
> - Partners switch roles.
> - Partners cut out their socks.

(?) **Do our socks need to look the same? Why?**

(?) **What can we draw on our socks? How many [triangles] will we draw on each sock? Where will we draw them?**

(?) **How many [triangles] did we draw all together on both socks? How can we find out?**

(?) **How did we share the work? How did we make sure our socks match?**

(¿) *¿Tienen nuestros calcetines que ser iguales? ¿Por qué?*

(¿) *¿Qué podemos dibujar en nuestros calcetines? ¿Cuántos [triángulos] dibujaremos en cada calcetín? ¿Dónde los dibujaremos?*

(¿) *¿Cuántos [triángulos] en total dibujamos en los dos calcetines? ¿Cómo lo podemos averiguar?*

(¿) *¿Cómo compartimos el trabajo? ¿Cómo nos aseguramos de que nuestros calcetines fueran iguales?*

Pair Work

1. Distribute materials to each pair.

2. Have pairs do the activity. Circulate and talk with pairs about their work and their thinking.

Children Working in Pairs

> **?** **How do you know that your socks match?**

> **?** **If you add another** [circle] **to your sock, how many** [circles] **will you have?**

> **?** **Do you have** [more circles] **or** [more stripes] **on your sock? How do you know?**

> **?** **How are you sharing the work? Do you both think that's fair?**

> **¿?** *¿Cómo saben que sus calcetines son iguales?*

> **¿?** *Si dibujan otro* [círculo] *en su calcetín, ¿cuántos* [círculos] *tendrán?*

> **¿?** *¿Tienen* [más círculos] *o* [más rayas] *en su calcetín? ¿Cómo lo saben?*

> **¿?** *¿Cómo están compartiendo el trabajo? ¿Piensan ambos que lo hacen de una manera justa?*

Report and Reflect

1. Collect the decorated socks and then randomly distribute one to each child.

2. Have children find and sit with the person who has a matching sock. Discuss:

Whole Class in Pairs

> **?** **How did you look for the sock that matches yours? How did you know when you found it?**

> **?** **What are some things that you can count on your sock? How many** [circles] **are on your sock? How many** [circles] **are on both of your socks?**

> **?** **You have** [six stripes] **all together on your two socks. How many** [stripes] **does each sock have? How do you know?**

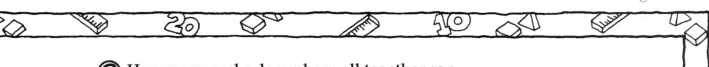

(?) How many socks do we have all together as a class? How can we find out?

(¿) *¿En qué se fijaron para buscar el calcetín igual al suyo? ¿Cómo supieron que lo habían encontrado?*

(¿) *¿Qué cosas pueden contar en su calcetín? ¿Cuántos [círculos] hay en su calcetín? ¿Cuántos [círculos] hay en los dos calcetines?*

(¿) *Tienen [seis rayas] en total en sus dos calcetines. ¿Cuántos [rayas] tiene cada calcetín? ¿Cómo lo saben?*

(¿) *¿Cuántos calcetines tiene en total toda la clase? ¿Cómo lo podemos averiguar?*

Prepare for Success at Home

I. Show and explain the **At Home** activity. Explain that children and their home partners will gather, match, and count the family's socks. Discuss:

Whole Class

(?) Who will you ask to be your home partner? If that person can't work with you, who is someone else you might ask?

(?) When is a good time to ask someone to be your home partner? Why is that a good time?

(¿) *¿A quién van a pedir que sea su compañero en casa? Si esa persona no puede trabajar con ustedes, ¿a quién más podrían pedírselo?*

(¿) *¿Cuándo es un buen momento para pedir que alguien sea su compañero en casa? ¿Por qué es ése un buen momento?*

2. Explain when children are to bring their At Home Activities back to class and that they will show the class the socks they drew at home. Discuss:

(?) How will you remember to bring your At Home activity back to school?

(¿) *¿Cómo van a recordar que tienen que traer su Actividad en casa a la escuela?*

BACK AT SCHOOL

Get Ready

1. Collect and review the **At Home** activities.

2. Determine how you will select partners.

Discuss the At Home Activity

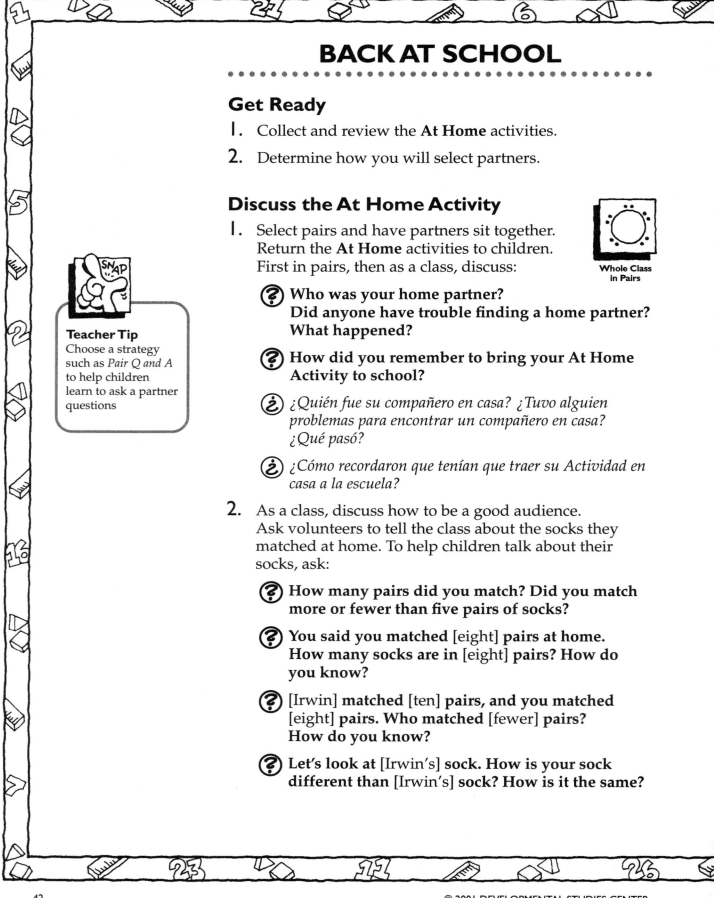

**Whole Class
in Pairs**

1. Select pairs and have partners sit together. Return the **At Home** activities to children. First in pairs, then as a class, discuss:

   (?) Who was your home partner? Did anyone have trouble finding a home partner? What happened?

   (?) How did you remember to bring your At Home Activity to school?

   (¿) *¿Quién fue su compañero en casa? ¿Tuvo alguien problemas para encontrar un compañero en casa? ¿Qué pasó?*

   (¿) *¿Cómo recordaron que tenían que traer su Actividad en casa a la escuela?*

2. As a class, discuss how to be a good audience. Ask volunteers to tell the class about the socks they matched at home. To help children talk about their socks, ask:

   (?) How many pairs did you match? Did you match more or fewer than five pairs of socks?

   (?) You said you matched [eight] pairs at home. How many socks are in [eight] pairs? How do you know?

   (?) [Irwin] matched [ten] pairs, and you matched [eight] pairs. Who matched [fewer] pairs? How do you know?

   (?) Let's look at [Irwin's] sock. How is your sock different than [Irwin's] sock? How is it the same?

Teacher Tip
Choose a strategy such as *Pair Q and A* to help children learn to ask a partner questions

(¿) *¿Cuántos pares emparejaste? ¿Emparejaste más o menos que cinco pares de calcetines?*

(¿) *Tú me dijiste que emparejaste [ocho] pares en casa. ¿Cuántos calcetines hay en [ocho] pares? ¿Cómo lo sabes?*

(¿) *[Irwin] emparejó [diez] pares, y tu emparejaste [ocho] pares. ¿Quién emparejó [menos] pares? ¿Cómo lo sabes?*

(¿) *Vamos a mirar el calcetín de [Irwin]. ¿En qué se diferencia tu calcetín del calcetín de [Irwin]? ¿En qué se parece?*

Extend the Experience

- Have children cut out the socks drawn on their **At Home** activities. As a class, sort the socks into groups.

- Hang the paper socks on a clothesline. As a class, count each sock as it is hung.

- Put the socks in a math center for children to sort according to the attributes the socks share, such as size, color, pattern, and number of designs.

- Ask children how they could form groups according to the attributes of the socks they are wearing. Try a variety of arrangements, such as children with patterned socks in one group and children with solid-colored socks in another.

Socks Pattern

Matching Socks

Dear Family,

Our class is learning about numbers. We decorated, matched, and counted pairs of paper socks. This activity helped us learn to:

- count and compare
- use math words such as *pair, match,* and *count.*

In this activity, the two of you will match and count pairs of your family's socks. You will draw one of the socks. In class, we will use the sock you draw for an activity.

① Collect the things you need.

- Eight to 10 pairs of socks
  (Find pairs that are as different as possible in color, size, and design.)
- A pencil
- Crayons or colored marking pens

② Talk about matching socks when folding the laundry.

③ Do the activity.

- Put the socks in a pile.

- Take turns looking through the pile to find pairs of socks.

- Count the pairs of socks.

Talk about:

- What did we find out?
- Do we have more plain socks or more socks with designs on them? How do you know?

4 Draw one of the socks and color in the details.

How many pairs of socks did you match? _____

5 Write your thoughts about this activity.

Dear Teacher:

_____

_____

_____

From, _____

(child's name)

_____

(home partner's name)

6 Get ready for school.
Talk about:

- What do you want to tell the class about what we did?

- What will help you remember to take this **At Home** activity back to class?

Emparejar calcetines

Estimada familia:

Nuestra clase está aprendiendo acerca de los números. Decoramos, emparejamos y contamos pares de calcetines de papel. Esta actividad nos ayudó a aprender a:

- contar y comparar
- usar palabras matemáticas como *par, emparejar y contar.*

En esta actividad, ustedes dos van a emparejar y a contar los pares de calcetines de su familia. Ustedes dibujarán uno de los calcetines. En clase, usaremos el calcetín que dibujaron para una actividad.

① Reúnan las cosas que necesiten.

- Ocho a 10 pares de calcetines (Busquen pares que sean tan diferentes en color, talla y diseño como sea posible.)
- Un lápiz
- Creyones o marcadores de colores

② Hablen sobre emparejar calcetines mientras doblan la ropa limpia.

③ Hagan la actividad.

- Coloquen los calcetines en un montón.

- Túrnense buscando pares de calcetines en el montón.

- Cuenten los pares de calcetines.

Hablen sobre:

- ¿Qué averiguamos?
- ¿Tenemos más calcetines sencillos o más calcetines con dibujos? ¿Cómo lo sabes?

MathLinks At Home Activity

47

4 Dibujen uno de los calcetines y coloreen los detalles.

¿Cuántos pares de calcetines emparejaron? _____

5 Escriban lo que piensan sobre esta actividad.

Estimado maestro:

_____

_____

_____

De, _____

(nombre del niño)

_____

(nombre del compañero en casa)

6 **Prepárense para la escuela. Hablen sobre:**

- ¿Qué quieres contar a la clase acerca de lo que hicimos?

- ¿Qué te ayudará a recordar a llevar de vuelta a clase esta Actividad en casa?

Clap and Clap

AT SCHOOL

Pairs play "Clap and Clap," a game that helps them count to ten.

AT HOME

Children and their home partners play "Clap and Clap" and write or draw about one of their games.

BACK AT SCHOOL

Children discuss the **At Home** activity and play a version of "Clap and Clap" as a group.

Learning About Number

In this activity, children:
- count to ten.

Learning to Work Together

In this activity, children:
- listen to a partner
- teach a game to a home partner.

Mathematical Vocabulary

add	sumar
total	total

AT SCHOOL

Get Ready

1. Determine how you will select partners. (See **Forming Pairs,** p. 20.)

2. Prepare materials:

   - A copy of the **At Home** activity, with the return date written on it, for each child

   - A copy of "Clap and Clap" Number Cards, p. 55, for each child, attached to the **At Home** activity

   - A paper bag containing a set of "Clap and Clap" Number Cards, p. 55, for each pair (Copy the number cards onto construction paper or card stock to make them more durable or use playing cards ace through nine.)

Explain and Model the Game

Whole Class in Pairs

1. Select pairs and have partners sit together. Explain that you will clap a secret number of times and that the class is to listen and then add claps until the total number of claps equals ten. Explain that to practice you will count aloud, but when pairs play, they will count silently. Pick a card from the bag and clap [five] times, counting each clap aloud. Ask the class to add enough claps to make ten claps, counting each clap aloud. Repeat several times. Each time, discuss:

   (?) **How many times did I clap? How did you know how many more to add?**

   (?) **How many times did we clap in total? How do you know?**

   (¿) *¿Cuántas veces aplaudí? ¿Cómo supieron cuántas veces más tenían que aplaudir?*

   (¿) *¿Cuántas veces aplaudimos en total? ¿Cómo lo saben?*

2. Choose a pair to demonstrate the game as you explain the directions one at a time. As the pair models, discuss with the class:

 Why is it important to take turns in this game? Why do you need to listen to your partner?

¿Por qué es importante turnarse en este juego? ¿Porqué necesitan escuchar a su compañero?

Pair Work

1. Distribute materials to each pair.

2. Have pairs play the game several times. Circulate and talk with pairs about the game and their thinking:

Children Working in Pairs

How do you know that your partner is listening while you are clapping?

How many times did your partner clap? How many times will you clap? How do you know?

¿Cómo saben que su compañero está escuchando mientras aplauden?

¿Cuántas veces aplaudió su compañero? ¿Cuántas veces aplaudirás tú? ¿Cómo lo sabes?

Report and Reflect

1. First in pairs, then as a class, discuss the game:

Whole Class in Pairs

What went well when you played the game? What problems did you have? How did you solve these problems?

How did you know your partner was paying attention while you were clapping?

After your partner clapped, how did you know the number of times to clap? Did anyone figure it out in a different way?

¿Qué salió bien cuando jugaron a este juego? ¿Qué problemas tuvieron? ¿Cómo resolvieron estos problemas?

"Clap and Clap" Directions

Goal: Partners clap a total of ten times.

1. Decide who will be first.

2. The first player draws a card from the bag and claps the number on the card (without showing the card to his or her partner or counting aloud).

3. The second player silently counts the claps and then claps the number of times needed to make a total of ten claps.

4. The first player returns the card to the bag.

5. The second player draws a card from the bag and claps the number on the card. The first player claps on to ten.

6. Play until all of the cards are drawn from the bag.

(¿) *¿Cómo supieron que su compañero estaba prestando atención mientras aplaudían?*

(¿) *Después de que su compañero aplaudió, ¿cómo supieron cuántas veces tenían que aplaudir? ¿Lo averiguó alguien de una manera diferente?*

2. Pick a pair and ask the partners to show one way they clapped to ten.

(?) **Did any pair clap to ten a different way? Show us.**

(?) **After listening to your partner clap, how did you know the number of times to clap?**

(¿) *¿Aplaudió alguna pareja de estudiantes hasta diez de una manera diferente? Muéstrennos.*

(¿) *Después de escuchar aplaudir a su compañero, ¿cómo supieron el número de veces que tenían que aplaudir?*

Prepare for Success at Home

1. Show and explain the **At Home** activity. Explain that children will teach their home partners how to play "Clap and Clap." Ask:

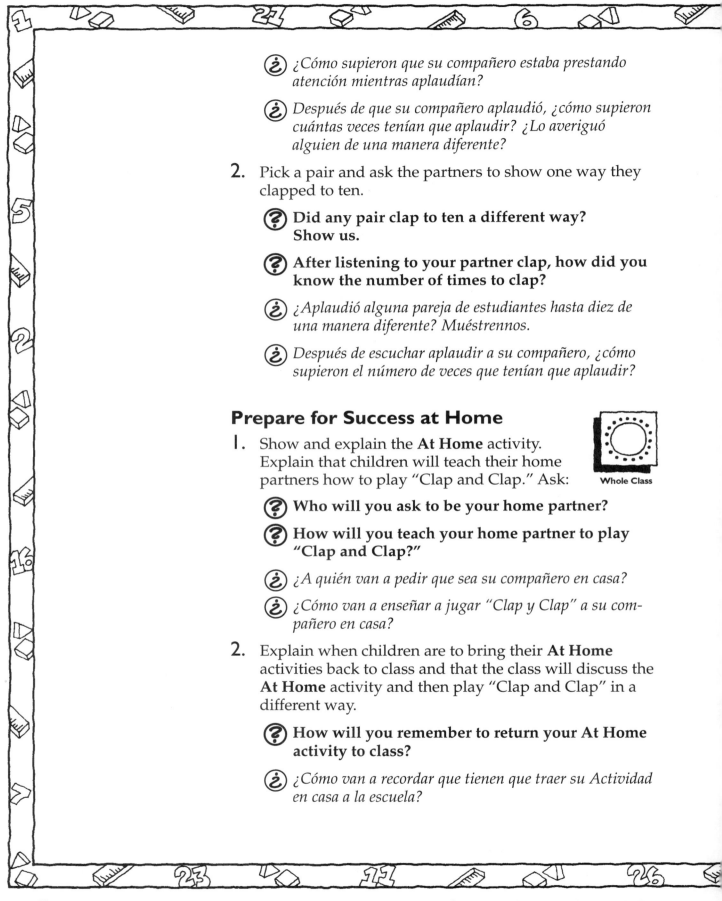

Whole Class

(?) **Who will you ask to be your home partner?**

(?) **How will you teach your home partner to play "Clap and Clap?"**

(¿) *¿A quién van a pedir que sea su compañero en casa?*

(¿) *¿Cómo van a enseñar a jugar "Clap y Clap" a su compañero en casa?*

2. Explain when children are to bring their **At Home** activities back to class and that the class will discuss the **At Home** activity and then play "Clap and Clap" in a different way.

(?) **How will you remember to return your At Home activity to class?**

(¿) *¿Cómo van a recordar que tienen que traer su Actividad en casa a la escuela?*

BACK AT SCHOOL

Get Ready

1. Collect and review the **At Home** activities.

2. Determine how you will select partners.

3. Prepare materials:

   - One set of number cards in a bag (from the **At School** activity)

Discuss the At Home Activity

Whole Class in Pairs

1. Select pairs and have partners sit together. Return the **At Home** activities to children. Have partners tell each other about playing "Clap and Clap" at home. After pairs discuss each question, discuss as a class.

   (?) **What was one way you and your partner clapped to ten?**

   (?) **What did you like about playing "Clap and Clap" with your home partner? What did you and your home partner find hard about playing "Clap and Clap"?**

   (?) **Did you think of another way to play "Clap and Clap"? How?**

   (¿) *¿Cuál fue una manera en la que ustedes y sus compañeros aplaudieron hasta diez?*

   (¿) *¿Qué les gustó de jugar a "Clap y Clap" con su compañero en casa? ¿Qué les pareció difícil a ustedes y a su compañero en casa de jugar a "Clap y Clap"?*

   (¿) *¿Pensaron en alguna otra manera de jugar a "Clap y Clap"? ¿Cómo?*

2. Explain that the class will play "Clap and Clap" together using other actions such as jumps, finger-snaps, head pats, or toe-taps. One at a time, ask children to draw a number from the bag, decide on an action, and then do it the number of times on the card. Ask the class to watch and listen, then continue the

Teacher Tip
Choose a strategy such as *Pair Q and A* to help children learn to ask a partner questions.

Teacher Tip
You might want to try some of the children's ideas for another way to play the game instead of or in addition to this game.

same action until the total reaches ten. (For example, a child draws a seven card and jumps seven times. The class responds by jumping three times to make ten.)

Extend the Experience

- Put the bags of number cards in a math center so that pairs can play during free-choice times.

- Play "Clap and Clap" with other numbers.

- Play "Clap and Clap" in groups of three. Have two children play while the third child records the combinations for ten that are clapped. Have children take turns playing and recording.

Directions: Cut or tear along the lines and put the number cards in a paper bag or container.

0	1	2	3
4	5	6	7
8	9	10	

"Clap and Clap" Number Cards   55

Instrucciones: Recorten o rasguen por las líneas y pongan las tarjetas con números en una bolsa de papel o en un recipiente.

0	1	2	3
4	5	6	7
8	9	10	

Clap and Clap

Dear Family,

Our class is learning about numbers. We played the game "Clap and Clap." This game helped us learn to:

- count to ten
- use math words such as *total*.

In this activity, the two of you will play "Clap and Clap." In class, we will play a new "Clap and Clap" game.

① Collect the things you need.

- A pencil, pen, or crayon
- A bag, hat, or other container
- The attached number cards 0-10 (tear or cut apart the cards)

② Talk about the game "Clap and Clap" played at school.

③ Play "Clap and Clap." The goal is to clap a total of ten times.

- Put the number cards in a paper bag or other container.
- Decide who will be first.
- The first player draws a card and, without showing the card to the other player, claps that number of times.

- The second player adds more claps so the total number of claps equals ten.

4 Take turns being first. Play until no cards are left. For one of the games, write the number of claps.

Child's Claps	Home Partner's Claps	Total number of Claps
___	___	___

5 Write your thoughts about this activity.

Dear Teacher:

_____

_____

_____

From, _____
(child's name)

_____
(home partner's name)

6 Get ready for school.
Talk about

• What did we learn playing this game together?
• What's another way to play this game that you could teach a partner at school?

Clap y Clap

Estimada familia:

Nuestra clase está aprendiendo acerca de los números.
Jugamos al juego "Clap y Clap". Este juego nos ayudó a
aprender a:

- contar hasta diez
- usar palabras matemáticas como *total*.

En esta actividad, ustedes dos jugarán a "Clap y Clap".
En clase, jugaremos a otro juego nuevo de "Clap y Clap".

❶ Reúnan las cosas que necesiten.

- Un lápiz, una pluma o un creyón
- Una bolsa, sombrero u otro recipiente
- Las tarjetas incluidas con números del 0 al 10
  (rasgue o recorte las tarjetas)

❷ Hablen sobre el juego de "Clap y Clap" al que jugaron en la escuela.

¿Cómo se juega a "Clap y Clap"?

Tomo una tarjeta y aplaudo ese número de veces. Después tú das más aplausos hasta hacer diez.

❸ Jueguen a "Clap y Clap." La meta es aplaudir un total de diez veces.

- Coloquen las tarjetas con números en una bolsa de papel o en un recipiente.
- Decidan quién irá primero.
- El primer jugador toma una tarjeta y, sin mostrársela al otro jugador, aplaude ese número de veces.

Uno, dos, tres...

Clap, Card Bag

- El segundo jugador da más aplausos para que el total de aplausos sea diez.

Cuatro, cinco, seis....

Clap, Card Bag

MathLinks At Home Activity

© 2001 DEVELOPMENTAL STUDIES CENTER   59

4 Túrnense siendo el primero. Jueguen hasta que no queden tarjetas. Para uno de los juegos, escriban el número de aplausos.

Aplausos del niño

_____

Aplausos del compañero en casa

_____

Número total de aplausos

_____

5 Escriban lo que piensan sobre esta actividad.

Estimado maestro:

_____
_____
_____
_____

De, _____
(nombre del niño)

_____
(nombre del compañero en casa)

6 Prepárense para la escuela.
Hablen sobre:

• ¿Qué aprendimos jugando juntos a este juego?

• ¿De qué otra forma se podría jugar a este juego para enseñársela a un compañero en la escuela?

Equal Groups

AT SCHOOL

Pairs play "Equal Groups," a game to determine whether groups of beans are equal or unequal.

AT HOME

Children and their home partners play "Equal Groups." They discuss the number of objects in each group and record the results of two of their turns.

BACK AT SCHOOL

Children determine the number of objects in a group without counting. First they use dots on a card, then drawings on their At Home Activities.

Learning About Number

In this activity, children:

- count
- compare two quantities
- recognize groups of objects without counting (*subitizing*).

Learning to Work Together

In this activity, children

- make decisions together.

Mathematical Vocabulary

equal	igual
unequal	desigual
fewer	menos
fewest	menor
compare	comparar

AT SCHOOL

Literature Link
Ten Black Dots by Donald Crews (Scholastic Inc., 1986). Introduce the activity with this book to help children understand the concept of a group. (optional)

Get Ready

1. Determine how you will select the partners who will work together. (See **Forming Pairs,** p. 20.)

2. Prepare materials:

   - A copy of the **At Home** activity, with the return date written on it for each child. A copy of "Equal Groups" Game Board, p. 67, for each child, attached to the **At Home** activity

   - A resealable plastic bag containing 6 paper cups and 18 beans (or objects of similar size) for each pair and the teacher

   - An "Equal Groups" Game Board, p. 67, for each pair

Make Connections

Whole Class in Pairs

1. Select pairs and have partners sit together. Show the class two groups of beans, each with four or fewer. Explore the concept of equal and unequal groups by discussing and comparing the two groups:

   (?) What can you tell us about these groups? Do they have the same number of beans in them? How do you know?

   (?) Does anyone know the word mathematicians use to describe groups that have the same number of objects?

   Teacher Tip
   If children do not know the terms, explain that mathematicians use the word *equal* to describe groups that have the same number of objects and *unequal* to describe groups that do not have the same number of objects.

   (¿) *¿Qué nos pueden decir sobre estos grupos? ¿Tienen el mismo número de frijoles? ¿Cómo lo saben?*

   (¿) *¿Sabe alguien la palabra que usan los matemáticos para describir grupos que tienen el mismo número de objetos?*

Explain and Model the Game

1. Explain that pairs will play "Equal Groups," a game to find groups with equal numbers of beans.

2. Choose a pair to demonstrate as you explain the game directions one at a time. As they model, discuss with the class:

(?) **How can** [Salim] **and** [Velma] **decide who is first? Is that fair? What's another way?**

(?) **How many beans did** [Salim] **find under the first cup? How many beans does** [Velma] **need to find to have equal groups?**

(?) **Is the number of beans under** [Salim's] **cup equal to the number of beans under** [Velma's] **cup? How do you know?**

(¿) *¿Cómo pueden* [Salim] *y* [Velma] *decidir quién irá primero? ¿Es eso justo? ¿Hay alguna otra manera? Si es así, ¿cuál es?*

(¿) *¿Cuántos frijoles encontró* [Salim] *debajo de la primera taza? ¿Cuántos frijoles necesita* [Velma] *para tener grupos iguales?*

(¿) *¿Es el número de frijoles que hay debajo de la taza de* [Salim] *igual al número de frijoles que hay debajo de la taza de* [Velma]? *¿Cómo lo saben?*

Pair Work

1. Distribute materials to each pair.

2. As a class, set up the game boards.

Children Working in Pairs

3. Have pairs play the game several times. Circulate and talk with them about the game and their thinking.

(?) **How do you know that the groups are equal?**

(?) (If groups are unequal) **Which group has more? How many more?**

(¿) *¿Cómo saben que los grupos son iguales?*

(¿) (Si los grupos son desiguales) *¿Qué grupo tiene más? ¿Cuántos más?*

"Equal Groups" Directions

Goal: Find groups of beans that are equal.

1. Set up the game board:
   • Put two beans in two of the circles, three beans in another two circles, and four beans in the final two circles.
   • Cover the groups of beans with cups and move the cups around to mix them up. Move the cups slowly, without tilting them, so that the beans stay underneath the cups.

2. Decide who will be first.

3. The first player lifts a cup, looks at the beans, and says the number.

4. The second player lifts another cup. If both groups have the same number of beans, the players say "Equal groups!" If not, they say "Unequal groups!"

5. If the groups are equal, players remove the beans and cups. If the groups are unequal, players put the cups back over them.

6. Switch roles and play again.

7. Continue playing until all the cups and beans have been removed from the game board.

Teacher Tip
Use a strategy such as *Think, Pair, Share* to give children time to think on their own before discussing their thinking with others.

Report and Reflect

1. First in pairs, then as a class, discuss the game:

Whole Class in Pairs

(?) How did you and your partner choose who was first? Did you both think that was fair? Why?

(?) What were two equal groups you found? How did you know? What were two unequal groups?

(¿) *¿Cómo decidieron tú y tu compañero quién iría primero? ¿Pensaron ambos que eso era justo? ¿Por qué?*

(¿) *¿Qué dos grupos iguales encontraron? ¿Cómo lo supieron? ¿Qué dos grupos desiguales encontraron?*

Prepare for Success at Home

1. Show and explain the **At Home** activity. Explain that children and their home partners will play "Equal Groups." Discuss:

Whole Class

(?) Who will you ask to work with you at home?

(?) What can you use at home if you don't have beans? What can you use instead of cups?

(?) What does "equal groups" mean?

(¿) *¿A quién van a pedir que trabaje con ustedes en casa?*

(¿) *¿Qué pueden usar en casa si no tienen frijoles? ¿Qué pueden usar en lugar de tazas?*

(¿) *¿Qué quiere decir "grupos iguales"?*

2. Explain when children are to bring their **At Home** activities back to class and that the class will use the information they write on their **At Home** activities to learn more about equal groups. Discuss:

(?) Where would be a good place to put the At Home activity when you finish it so that you will remember to bring it back to school?

(¿) *¿Cuál sería un buen lugar para colocar la Actividad en casa cuando terminen para que se acuerden de traerla a clase?*

BACK AT SCHOOL

Get Ready

1. Collect and review the **At Home** activities. Look at what is written in Box #4 and select several to show the class. Fold them so that only the record of the two turns is showing. You may want to make an enlarged copy or a transparency to make them easier to see.

2. Determine how you will select partners.

3. Prepare materials:

   • Set of Dot Pattern Cards, pp. 68–80.

Discuss the At Home Activity

1. Select pairs and have partners sit together. Return the **At Home** activities to children. First in pairs, then as a class, discuss:

   ? **When did you play "Equal Groups" at home? Was that a good time? Why?**

   ? **What went well? What problems did you have? Were you able to solve them? How?**

   ¿? *¿Cuándo jugaron a "Grupos iguales" en casa? ¿Se divirtieron? ¿Por qué?*

   ¿? *¿Qué salió bien? ¿Qué problemas tuvieron? ¿Fueron capaces de resolverlos? ¿Cómo?*

Whole Class in Pairs

Teacher Tip
Use a strategy such as *Turn to Your Partner* to give all children a chance to think and talk about the questions.

2. Explain that one reason to play "Equal Groups" is to learn to see the number in a small group without counting. Show the dot cards and explain that you have another game that will help children learn to do this.

   Show one dot card for a few seconds, then hide it. Ask children to hold up their fingers to show you the number of dots they saw. Repeat several times using different dot cards. Each time, ask several children:

   ? **How many dots are in this group? How do you know?**

   ¿? *¿Cuántos puntos hay en este grupo? ¿Cómo lo saben?*

3. Explain that you will show the groups what some children recorded on their **At Home** activity. Ask children to decide whether the groups are equal. Show one of the folded **At Home** activities for a few seconds. Ask:

> **(?)** **Are the groups equal or unequal? How do you know?**

> **(¿)** *¿Son los grupos iguales o desiguales? ¿Cómo lo saben?*

If the two groups are unequal, ask:

> **(?)** **Which group has more [beans]? Which has fewer? How could we make these groups equal?**

> **(¿)** *¿Qué grupo tiene más [frijoles] ¿Cuál tiene menos? ¿Cómo podemos hacer estos grupos iguales?*

Repeat with several other folded **At Home** activities.

4. Discuss the importance of having the **At Home** activity for the **Back at School** activity and thank children for returning them. Discuss:

> **(?)** **How did we use the At Home activity in class?**

> **(?)** **What mathematics did we do today?**

> **(¿)** *¿Cómo usamos la Actividad en casa en la clase?*

> **(¿)** *¿Qué matemáticas hicimos hoy?*

Extend the Experience

- Have one partner place some beans in one of the circles on the game board. Have the other partner make an equal group in another circle. Ask partners to check the groups to be sure that they are equal. If the groups are unequal, ask partners to agree how to make the groups equal. When they agree, have them remove the beans and switch roles.

- Play "Equal Groups" using groups of four, five, and six beans.

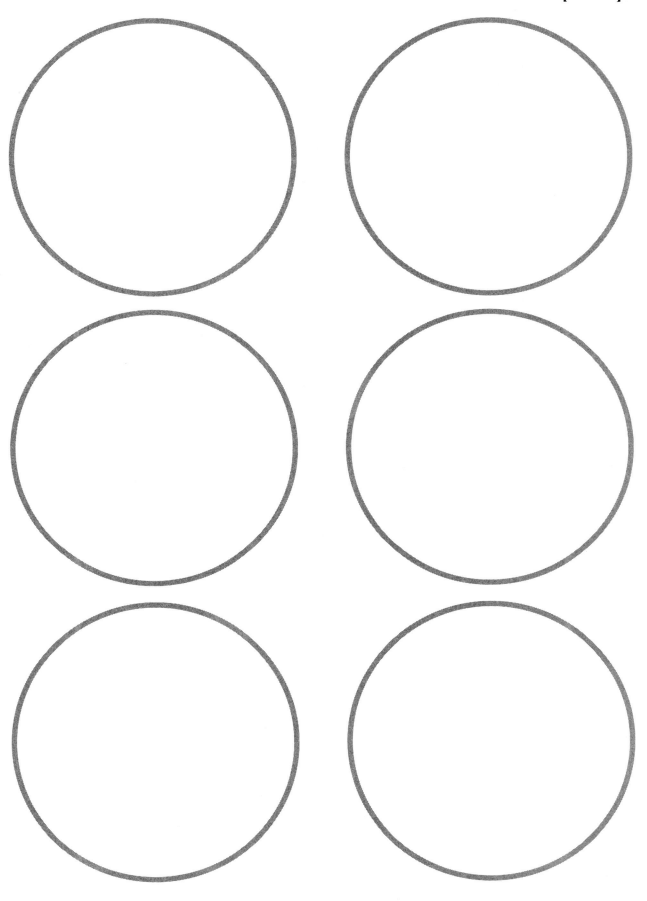

"Equal Groups" Game Board

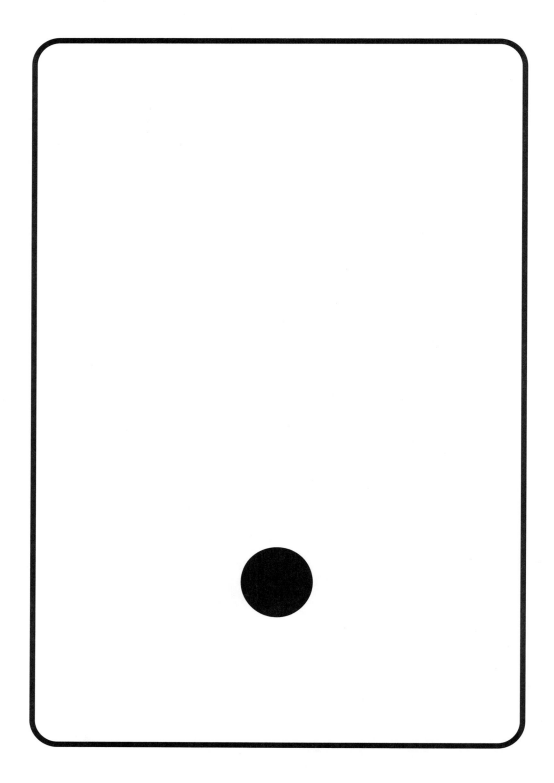

Dot Pattern Cards

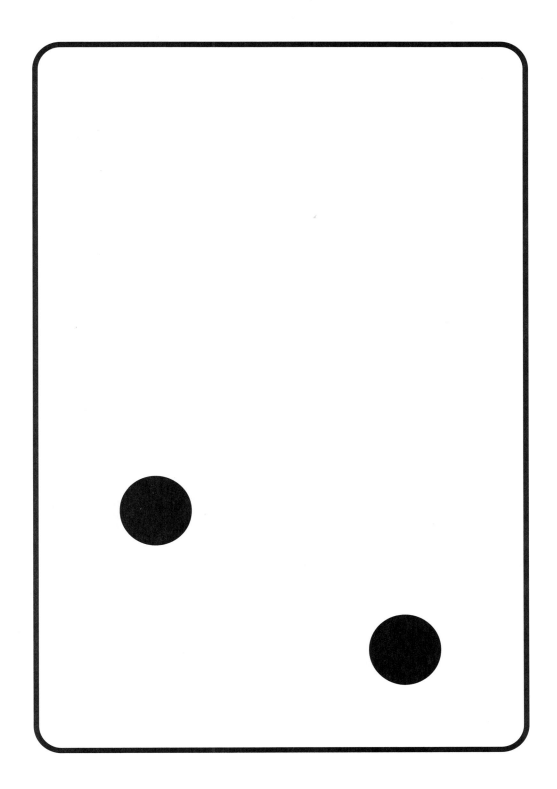

Dot Pattern Cards

Dot Pattern Cards

Dot Pattern Cards

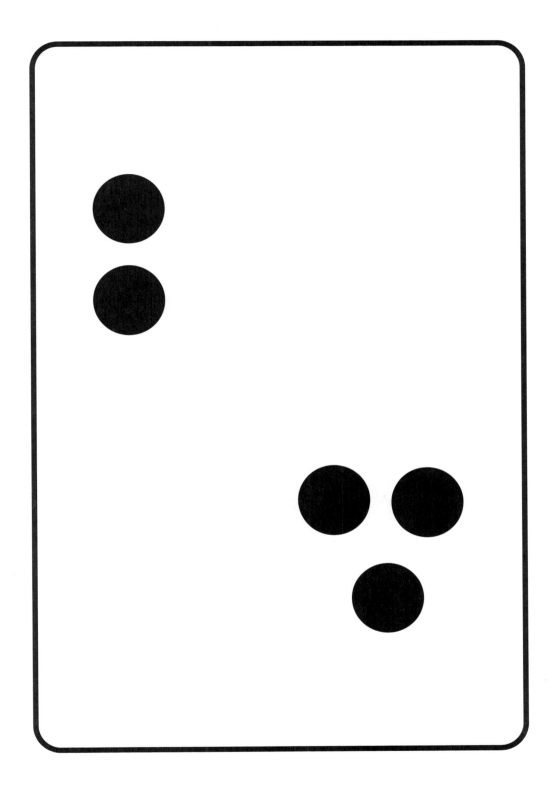

Dot Pattern Cards

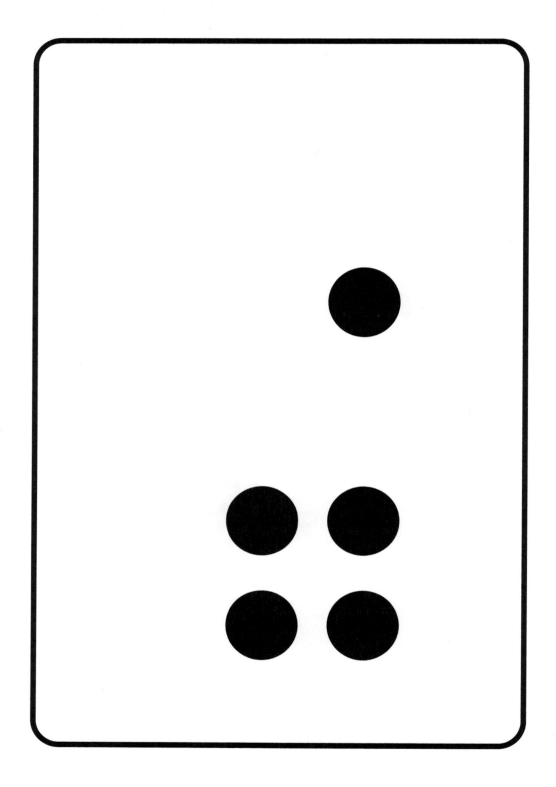

Dot Pattern Cards

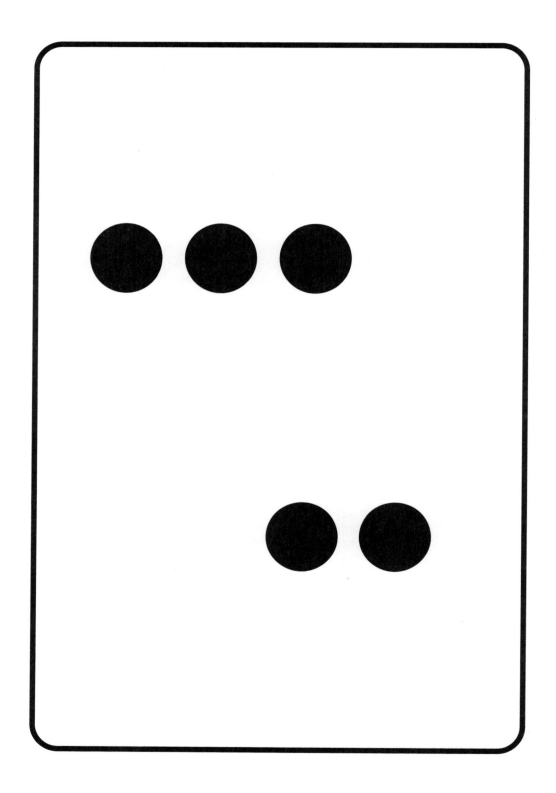

Dot Pattern Cards

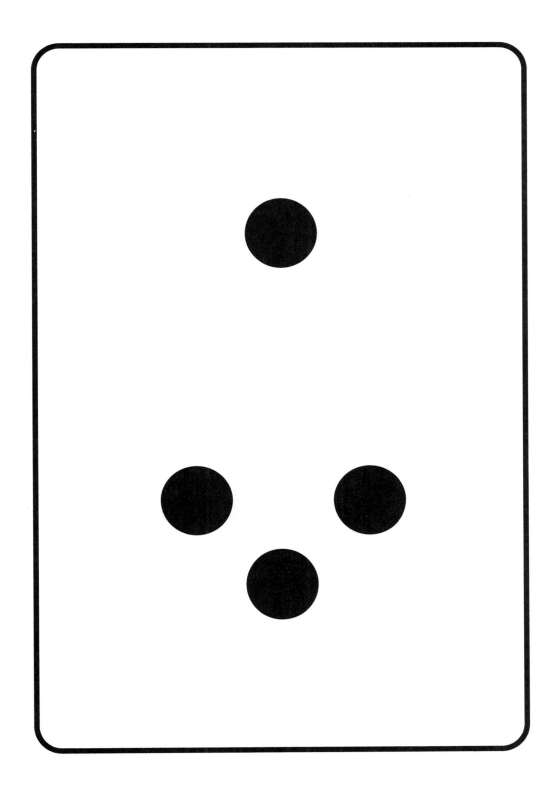

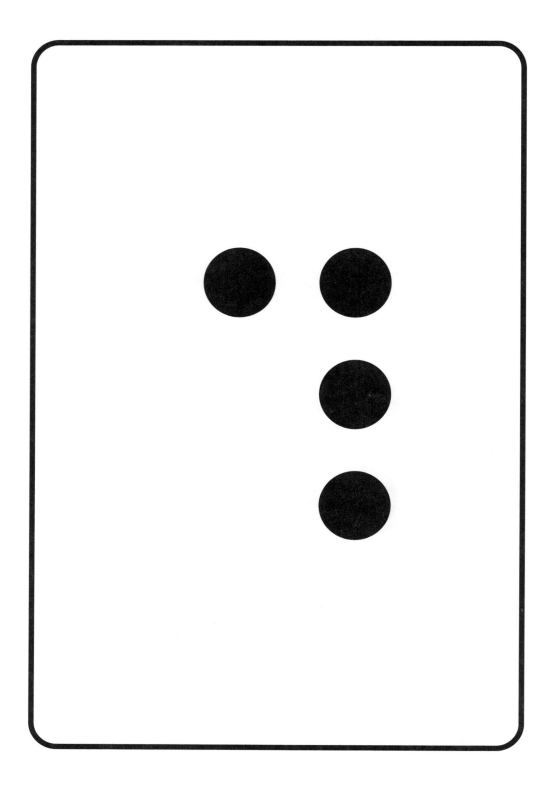

Dot Pattern Cards

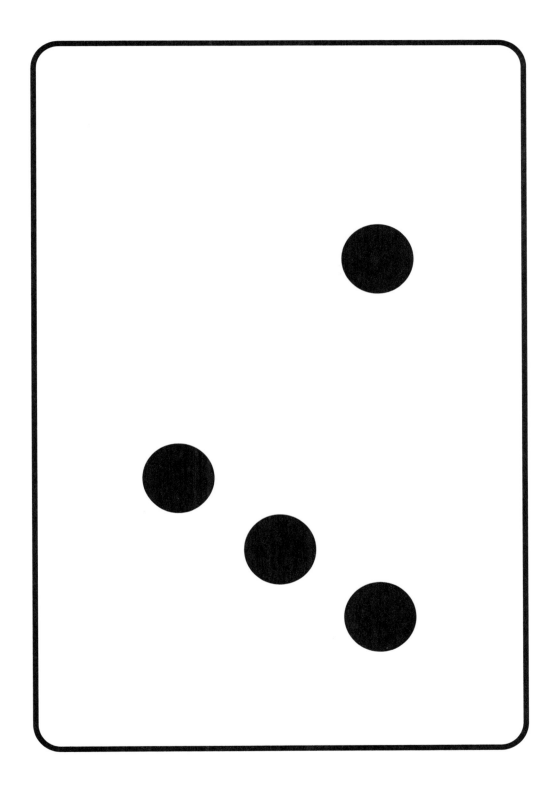

Dot Pattern Cards

Equal Groups

Dear Family,

Our class is learning about numbers. We played the game "Equal Groups." This game helped us learn to:

- identify equal and unequal groups
- use math words such as *fewer* and *unequal*.

In this activity, the two of you will play "Equal Groups" and draw pictures of two of your turns. In class, we will talk about the pictures.

❶ Collect the things you need.
- A pencil, pen, or crayon
- Eighteen small objects (beans, pennies, buttons)
- Six cups or other containers that you cannot see through
- The attached "Equal Groups" Game Board

❷ Set up the game board.
- Put the beans on the game board as shown.

- Cover each group of beans with a cup. Move the cups around to mix them up.

❸ Play "Equal Groups." The goal is to find groups of beans that are equal.

- Decide who will be first.
- The first player lifts a cup, looks at the beans, and says the number of beans.
- The second player lifts another cup. If both groups have the same number of beans, together say "Equal groups!" If not, say "Unequal groups!"
- When you find equal groups, remove the beans and cups. If the groups are unequal, put the cups back over them.
- Continue playing until all the cups and beans have been removed from the game board.

4 **Play again. Draw the beans you uncover during two of your turns.**

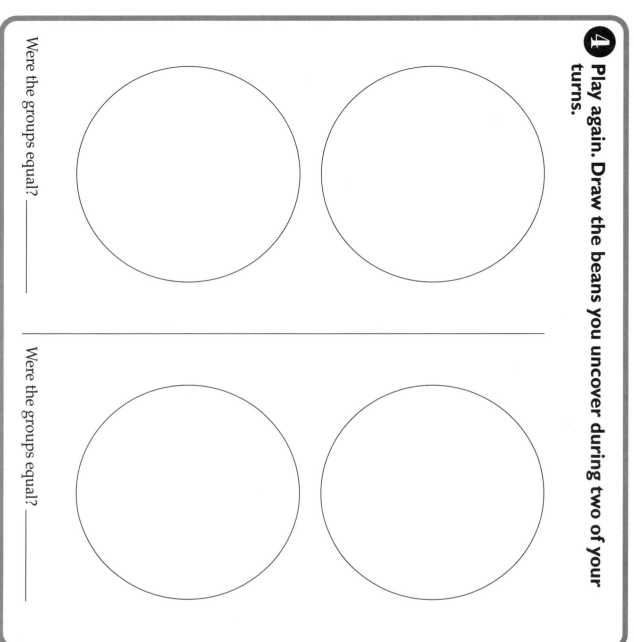

Were the groups equal? _____

Were the groups equal? _____

5 **Write your thoughts about this activity.**

Dear Teacher:

_____

_____

_____

From, _____

(child's name)

_____

(home partner's name)

6 **Get ready for school. Talk about:**

• How did we know when the groups were equal?

• When is a time when we need to count?

Grupos iguales

Estimada familia:

Nuestra clase está aprendiendo acerca de los números. Jugamos al juego "Grupos iguales". Este juego nos ayudó a aprender a:

- identificar grupos iguales y desiguales
- usar palabras matemáticas como *menos* y *desigual*.

En esta actividad, ustedes de dos jugarán a "Grupos iguales" y harán dibujos de dos de sus turnos. En clase, hablaremos de los dibujos.

① Reúnan las cosas que necesiten.

- Un lápiz, una pluma o un creyón
- Diez y ocho objetos pequeños (frijoles, centavos, botones)
- Seis tazas u otro recipiente que no sea transparente
- El tablero de juego incluido de "Grupos iguales"

② Preparen el tablero de juego.

- Pongan los frijoles en el tablero de juego como se muestra.

- Tapen cada grupo de frijoles con una taza. Muevan las tazas para mezclarlas.

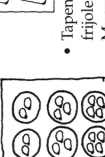

③ Jueguen a "Grupos iguales." La meta es encontrar grupos de frijoles que sean iguales.

- Decidan quién irá primero.

- El primer jugador levanta una taza, mira los frijoles y dice el número de frijoles.

- El segundo jugador levanta otra taza. Si los dos grupos tienen el mismo número de frijoles, digan juntos: "¡Grupos iguales!" Si no, digan: "¡Grupos desiguales!"

- Cuando encuentren grupos iguales, retiren los frijoles y las tazas. Si los grupos son desiguales, pongan las tazas de nuevo sobre los frijoles.

- Continúen jugando hasta que hayan retirado todas las tazas y los frijoles del tablero de juego.

4 Jueguen otra vez. Dibujen los frijoles que destapen durante dos de sus turnos.

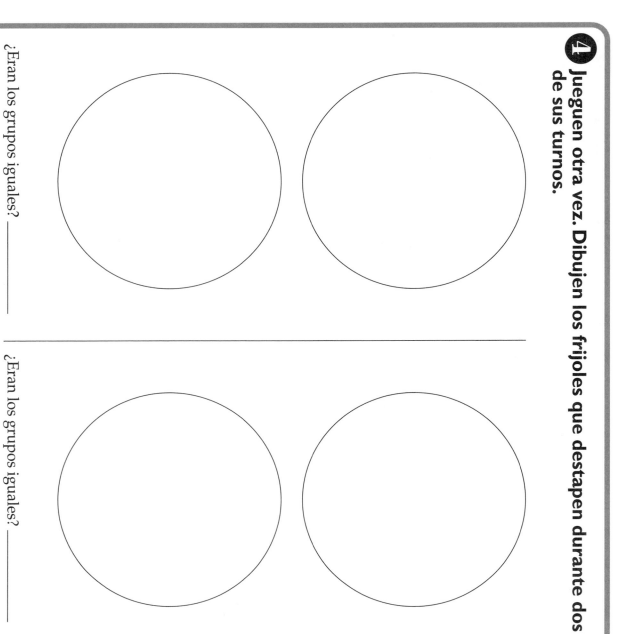

¿Eran los grupos iguales? _____

¿Eran los grupos iguales? _____

5 Escriban lo que piensan sobre esta actividad.

Estimado maestro:

_____

_____

_____

De, _____

(nombre del niño)

(nombre del compañero en casa)

6 Prepárense para la escuela. Hablen sobre:

• ¿Cómo supimos que los grupos eran iguales?

• ¿En qué momento tenemos que contar?

Penny Towers

AT SCHOOL

Partners play the game "Penny Towers," tossing a penny to determine if they can add a penny to their tower. When they run out of pennies or the tower falls, partners count the number of pennies in their tower.

AT HOME

Children and their home partners play "Penny Towers" and record their results.

BACK AT SCHOOL

Pairs discuss their results from home.

Learning About Number

In this activity, children:

- count using one-to-one correspondence
- compare quantities.

Learning to Work Together

In this activity, children:

- share the work.

Mathematical Vocabulary

shortest	el más bajo
tallest	el más alto
most	la mayoría
same	igual

AT SCHOOL

"Penny Towers" Directions

Goal: Stack as many pennies as possible before the tower falls over or no more pennies are left.

1. Decide who will be first.

2. The first player takes a penny from the bag, shakes it in the cup, and tosses it on the desk or table.

3. If the penny lands "heads up," the player uses it to begin to build the tower. If it lands "tails up," the player puts the penny back into the bag.

4. The second player takes a turn.

5. Take turns until the tower falls over or no pennies are left. (Players should not straighten the tower at any time.)

6. Count the number of pennies in the tower.

7. Play again.

Get Ready

1. Determine how you will select partners. (See **Forming Pairs,** p. 20.)

2. Prepare materials:

   • A copy of the **At Home** activity, with the return date written on it, for each child

   • Twenty pennies in a resealable plastic bag for each pair

   • A paper cup for each pair

Explain and Model the Game

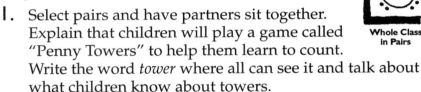

Whole Class in Pairs

1. Select pairs and have partners sit together. Explain that children will play a game called "Penny Towers" to help them learn to count. Write the word *tower* where all can see it and talk about what children know about towers.

2. Choose a pair to demonstrate the game as you explain the directions one at a time. As the pair models the game, discuss with the class:

   (?) How do we know if the penny is showing heads or tails?

   (?) The penny landed ["heads up"]**, so what should this pair do?**

   (¿) *¿Cómo sabemos si el centavo muestra cara o cruz?*

   (¿) *El centavo cayó* [en cara], *entonces ¿qué debe hacer esta pareja de estudiantes?*

   When the tower falls over or the pair runs out of pennies, discuss:

   (?) How can this pair find the number of pennies in their tower? How can they count the pennies so that they know they have counted all of them? Is there another way?

(?) How did [Andrea] and [Leslie] **work together to build their tower? How did they share the work of counting the pennies?**

(¿) *¿Cómo puede esta pareja de estudiantes averiguar el número de centavos que hay en su torre? ¿Cómo pueden contar todos los centavos y saber que los han contado todos? ¿Hay otra manera de hacerlo?*

(¿) *¿Cómo trabajaron [Andrea] y [Leslie] para construir su torre? ¿Cómo compartieron el trabajo de contar los centavos?*

Pair Work

1. Distribute materials to each pair.

2. Have pairs play the game several times. Circulate and talk with them about their work and their thinking:

Children Working in Pairs

(?) **How are you sharing the work?**

(?) **How many pennies do you think you have in this tower? Why do you say that?**

(¿) *¿Cómo están compartiendo el trabajo?*

(¿) *¿Cuántos centavos piensan que tienen en esta torre? ¿Por qué dicen eso?*

Report and Reflect

1. First in pairs, then as a class, discuss the game.

Whole Class in Pairs

(?) **How did you and your partner work together to build your towers? What problems did you have? How did you solve them?**

(?) **How did you count your pennies? What's another way?**

(?) **How many pennies were in one of your towers? Did any pair have a tower with [more] pennies? How do you know your tower had [more] pennies?**

> **Teacher Tip**
> Use a strategy such as *Turn to Your Partner* to give all of the children a chance to think and talk about the questions.

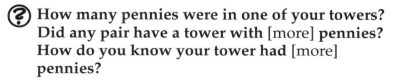
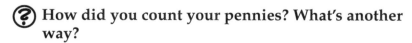

(?) Did any pair use all of your pennies? How many were there? How did you count them?

(¿) *¿Cómo trabajaron tú y tu compañero para construir sus torres? ¿Qué problemas tuvieron? ¿Cómo los resolvieron?*

(¿) *¿Cómo contaron sus centavos? ¿Hay otra manera más de contarlos? Si es así, ¿cuál es?*

(¿) *¿Cuántos centavos había en una de sus torres? ¿Había alguna pareja de estudiantes cuya torre tuviera [más] centavos? ¿Cómo saben que su torre tenía [más] centavos?*

(¿) *¿Usó alguna pareja de estudiantes todos sus centavos? ¿Cuántos había? ¿Cómo los contaron?*

Prepare for Success at Home

1. Show and explain the **At Home** activity. Explain that children and their home partners will play "Penny Towers." Discuss:

   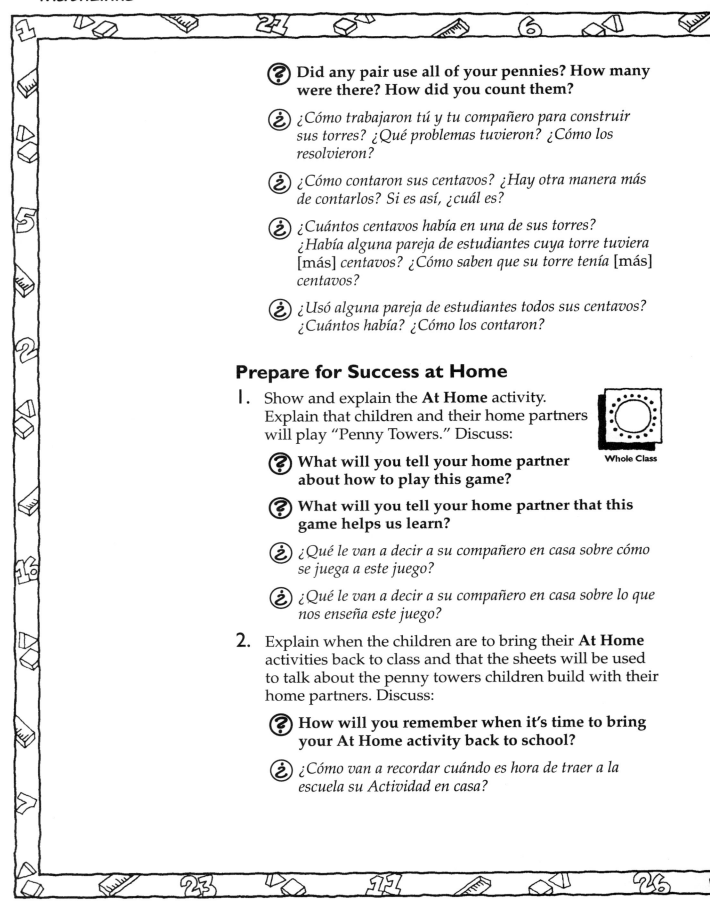

   Whole Class

   (?) What will you tell your home partner about how to play this game?

   (?) What will you tell your home partner that this game helps us learn?

   (¿) *¿Qué le van a decir a su compañero en casa sobre cómo se juega a este juego?*

   (¿) *¿Qué le van a decir a su compañero en casa sobre lo que nos enseña este juego?*

2. Explain when the children are to bring their **At Home** activities back to class and that the sheets will be used to talk about the penny towers children build with their home partners. Discuss:

   (?) How will you remember when it's time to bring your At Home activity back to school?

   (¿) *¿Cómo van a recordar cuándo es hora de traer a la escuela su Actividad en casa?*

BACK AT SCHOOL

Get Ready

1. Collect and review the **At Home** activities.

2. Determine how you will select partners.

Discuss the At Home Activity

1. Select pairs and have partners sit together. Return the **At Home** activities to children. First in pairs, then as a class, discuss:

(?) **How many pennies were in your towers?**

(?) **Who had a tower with more than fifteen pennies? How many were in your tower?**

(?) **Who had a tower with fewer than fifteen pennies? How many were in your tower?**

(?) **How did you remember to return your At Home Activity to school?**

(¿) *¿Cuántos centavos había en sus torres?*

(¿) *¿Quién tuvo una torre con más de quince centavos? ¿Cuántos había en tu torre?*

(¿) *¿Quién tenía una torre con menos de quince centavos? ¿Cuántos había en tu torre?*

(¿) *¿Cómo se acordaron de traer a la escuela su Actividad en casa?*

Extend the Experience

- Play "Build a Village" in the same way as "Penny Towers," but build "houses" made of five pennies. Once a house has five pennies, start a new house, continuing until all of the pennies have been used. When the village is built, have children count the pennies—counting by fives, if possible.

- Start a class penny collection to donate to a cause at the end of the school year. Have the class decide how to collect the pennies and where to donate them.

 **Penny Towers**

Dear Family,

Our class is learning about numbers. We played the game "Penny Towers." We built and counted towers of pennies. This game helped us learn to:

- count to 20
- use math words such as *fewest, same, tallest,* and *shortest.*

In this activity, the two of you will play "Penny Towers" and record your results. In class, we will discuss the towers you build.

① Collect the things you need.
- Twenty pennies
- A small cup
- A pencil, pen, or crayon

② Talk about playing "Penny Towers" at school.

Tell me about playing penny towers at school.

We made a tower that was seventeen pennies tall!

③ Play "Penny Towers." The goal is to stack as many pennies as possible before the tower falls over or no pennies are left.

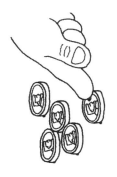

- Decide who will be first.
- The first player takes a penny, shakes it in the cup, and tosses it onto the table.

- If the penny lands "heads up," the player places it on the tower. If it lands "tails up," the player puts it back with the other pennies.

- The second player takes a turn.
- Take turns until the tower falls over or no pennies are left.
- Count the pennies in the tower.

4 Play "Penny Towers" three more times. Draw your penny towers and write the number of pennies in each.

Penny Tower 1

_____ Pennies

Penny Tower 2

_____ Pennies

Penny Tower 3

_____ Pennies

5 Write your thoughts about this activity.

Dear Teacher:

_____

_____

_____

From, _____
(child's name)

_____
(home partner's name)

6 Get ready for school. Talk about:

• How many pennies were in our tallest tower?

• What do you want to tell the class about our games?

Torres de centavos

Estimada familia:

Nuestra clase está aprendiendo acerca de los números. Jugamos al juego "Torres de centavos." Construimos y contamos torres de centavos. Este juego nos ayudó a aprender a:

- contar hasta 20
- usar palabras matemáticas como *el que menos, igual, el más alto y el más bajo.*

En esta actividad, ustedes dos van a jugar a "Torres de centavos" y van a anotar sus resultados. En clase, conversaremos sobre las torres que construyeron.

1 Reúnan las cosas que necesiten.

- Veinte monedas de 1 centavo
- Una taza pequeña
- Un lápiz, una pluma o un creyón

2 Hablen sobre el juego "Torres de centavos" al que jugaron en la escuela.

Cuéntame cómo jugaste a "Torres de centavos en la escuela.

¡Hicimos una torre 17 centavos de alta!

3 Jueguen a "Torres de centavos." La meta es amontonar tantos centavos como sea posible hasta que la torre se derrumbe o no queden más centavos.

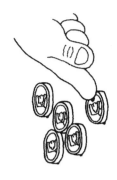

- Decidan quién irá primero.
- El primer jugador toma un centavo, lo pone en la taza, la agita y tira el centavo sobre la mesa.

- Si el centavo cae en "cara", el jugador lo pone sobre la torre. Si cae en "cruz", el jugador lo pone con el resto de los centavos.

- El segundo jugador toma su turno.
- Túrnense hasta que la torre se derrumbe o no queden más centavos.
- Cuenten los centavos en la torre.

4 Jueguen a "Torres de centavos" tres veces más. Dibujen sus torres de centavos y escriban el número de centavos en cada una.

Torre de centavos 1

_____ Centavos

Torre de centavos 2

_____ Centavos

Torre de centavos 3

_____ Centavos

5 Escriban lo que piensan sobre esta actividad.

Estimado maestro:

_____

_____

_____

De, _____

(nombre del niño)

_____

(nombre del compañero en casa)

6 Prepárense para la escuela. Hablen sobre:

- ¿Cuántos centavos había en nuestra torre más alta?

- ¿Qué quieres contar a la clase sobre nuestros juegos?

Number Drop

AT SCHOOL

In pairs, children play "Number Drop," taking turns dropping five cubes onto a circle and finding the number that fall inside and fall outside the circle. Pairs record the results of their final game.

AT HOME

Children and their home partners play "Number Drop" and record the results of four games.

BACK AT SCHOOL

In pairs, children talk about their work at home. The class uses this information to make a chart with the number combinations for five.

Learning About Number

In this activity, the children:

- compare quantities
- recognize groups of objects without counting (*subitizing*)
- explore number combinations that equal five.

Learning to Work Together

In this activity, the children:

- make decisions together.

Mathematical Vocabulary

same	igual
plus	más
line	línea

AT SCHOOL

Get Ready

1. Determine how you will select partners. (See **Forming Pairs,** p. 20.)

2. Prepare materials:

   - A copy of the **At Home** activity, with the return date written on it, for each child.

   - A copy of "Number Drop" Game Board, p. 101 for each child, attached to the **At Home** activity

   - "Number Drop" Game Board for each pair and one for modeling

   - Five cubes, or objects of similar size, for each pair

   - A pencil for each pair

Make Connections

Whole Class in Pairs

1. Select pairs and have partners sit together. Ask partners to tell each other what they know about the number five. First in pairs, then as a class, discuss:

   (?) What do you know about the number five?

   (?) What do you know about numbers that are less than five? more than five?

   (¿) ¿Qué saben acerca del número cinco?

   (¿) ¿Qué saben de los números menores que cinco? ¿De los mayores que cinco?

Explain and Model the Game

1. Explain that children will play a game to explore ways to make five. Choose a pair to demonstrate as you explain the directions one at a time. As the pair models the game, discuss with the class:

   (?) Did more cubes land inside the circle or outside the circle? How do you know?

"Number Drop" Game Directions

Goal: Drop five objects on the game board and find the number that land inside the circle and that land outside the circle.

1. Decide who will be first and how many turns to take.

2. The first player drops the five cubes onto the circle.

3. Together, say the number of cubes that fell inside the circle and outside the circle.

4. Take the cubes off of the game board.

5. The second player takes a turn.

6. Continue taking turns dropping the cubes.

7. Record the final game on the game board.

(?) [Two] **cubes landed inside the circle and** [three] **cubes landed outside the circle. How many cubes are there in total? Why do you think that?**

(?) **What should we do if a cube lands on the line? Should we say that it is inside or outside of the circle?**

(?) **How can we record the last game on this game board? What is another way?**

(¿) *¿Cayeron más cubos dentro del círculo o fuera del círculo? ¿Cómo lo saben?*

(¿) *[Dos] cubos cayeron dentro del círculo y [tres] cubos cayeron fuera del círculo. ¿Cuántos cubos hay en total? ¿Por qué piensan eso?*

(¿) *¿Qué debemos hacer si un cubo cae sobre la línea? ¿Debemos decir que está dentro o fuera del círculo?*

(¿) *¿Cómo podemos anotar el último juego en este tablero de juego? ¿Hay otra manera de hacerlo?*

Pair Work

1. Distribute materials to each pair.

2. Have pairs play the game several times, recording the results of their final game. Circulate and talk with them about their work and their thinking:

Children Working in Pairs

(?) **How many cubes landed inside the circle? How many landed outside the circle?**

(?) **What decisions are you making together? How are you making them?**

(¿) *¿Cuántos cubos cayeron dentro del círculo? ¿Cuántos cayeron fuera del círculo?*

(¿) *¿Qué decisiones están tomando juntos? ¿Cómo las están tomando?*

Teacher Tip
To give everyone enough time to finish, alert pairs when it is time to record the final game.

Report and Reflect

Whole Class in Pairs

1. As a class, discuss the results pairs recorded. Ask a few pairs to show their game boards and describe their drops. Discuss:

(?) [Jessica and Geoffrey] **dropped** [three] **cubes inside the circle and** [two] **outside the circle. They recorded their results like this. What is another way to record this game?**

(?) (Showing a pair's game board.) [Pablo and Natisha] **recorded these results. What do you know about their drop?**

(?) **Does anybody have a different combination of five cubes? What is it?**

(?) **How did you decide on the way you recorded your final game?**

(¿) [Jessica y Geoffrey] *dejaron caer* [tres] *cubos dentro del círculo y* [dos] *fuera del círculo. Anotaron sus resultados de esta manera. ¿De qué otra manera se puede anotar este juego?*

(¿) (Mostrando el tablero de juego de una pareja de estudiantes.) [Pablo y Natisha] *anotaron estos resultados. ¿Qué saben sobre sus resultados?*

(¿) *¿Tiene alguien una combinación distinta de cinco cubos? ¿Cuál es?*

(¿) *¿Cómo decidieron la manera de anotar su juego final?*

Prepare for Success at Home

Whole Class

1. Show and explain the **At Home** activity. Explain that children and their home partners will play "Number Drop." Discuss:

(?) **What do you have at home that you can drop instead of cubes? What else can you use?**

(?) **What helps you remember to take your At Home Activity home?**

(¿) *¿Qué tienen en casa para usar en este juego en lugar de cubos? ¿Qué más pueden usar?*

(¿) *¿Qué les ayuda a recordar que tienen que llevar a casa la Actividad en casa?*

2. Explain when the children are to bring their **At Home** activities back to class and that their work will be used to make a chart of the different number combinations for five. Discuss:

(?) **What helps you remember to bring your At Home activity back to school?**

(¿) *¿Qué les ayuda a recordar que tienen que traer a la escuela la Actividad en casa?*

BACK AT SCHOOL

Get Ready

1. Collect and review the **At Home** activity sheets.

2. Determine how you will select partners.

3. Prepare materials:

   - Six "Number Drop" game boards drawn or glued onto a chart or taped to the board

   - A marker for the teacher

Discuss the At Home Activity

Whole Class in Pairs

1. Select pairs and have partners sit together. Return the **At Home** activities to children. Have partners tell each other about the **At Home** activity.

   (?) **How did you and your home partner decide who would be first? How did that work?**

   (?) **What's one of the combinations for five that you found?**

   (¿) *¿Cómo decidieron tú y tu compañero en casa quién iría primero? ¿Cómo funcionó?*

(¿) *¿Cuál es una de las combinaciones de cinco que encontraron?*

2. Have several children report the results of the games recorded on their **At Home** activities. As they report a drop, record the numbers on a posted blank game board. Continue until you have written all of the number combinations that equal five. Discuss:

(?) **How can I record your drop on our chart? Is there another way?**

(?) **Does anyone have a drop that we do not have on our chart?**

(?) **What combinations did we find that equal five? How many combinations are there?**

(¿) *¿Cómo puedo anotar sus resultados en nuestra tabla?*

(¿) *¿Tiene alguien un resultado que no tenemos en nuestra tabla?*

(¿) *¿Qué combinaciones encontramos que forman cinco? ¿Cuántas combinaciones hay?*

Extend the Experience

- Play "Number Drop" and record the objects that fall on the line as a separate group. Have children write a number sentence on the game board for each drop. For example: for a drop with one cube on the line, two cubes inside the circle, and two cubes outside the circle, children could write $1 + 2 + 2 = 5$.

"Number Drop" Game Board   101

Child's Name: _____

Return Date: _____

Number Drop

Dear Family,

Our class is learning about the number five. We played the game "Number Drop." This game helped us learn to:

- find different number combinations that equal five
- use math words such as *combination, equal,* and *plus.*

In this activity, the two of you will play "Number Drop." In class, we will discuss the combinations that you find.

① Collect the things you need.

- Five beans or other small objects that do not roll, such as macaroni, pennies, or buttons
- A pencil
- The attached "Number Drop" Game Board

② Talk about playing "Number Drop" at school.

③ Play "Number Drop."

The goal is to count the number of objects that land inside and outside the circle.

- Decide who will be first.
- The first player drops the five objects onto the game board.

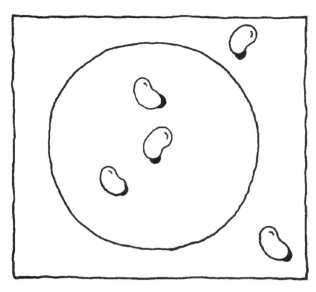

- Together, count the number of objects that land inside and outside the circle.

MathLinks At Home Activity

4 Play "Number Drop" four more times. Draw a picture or use numbers to show each drop.

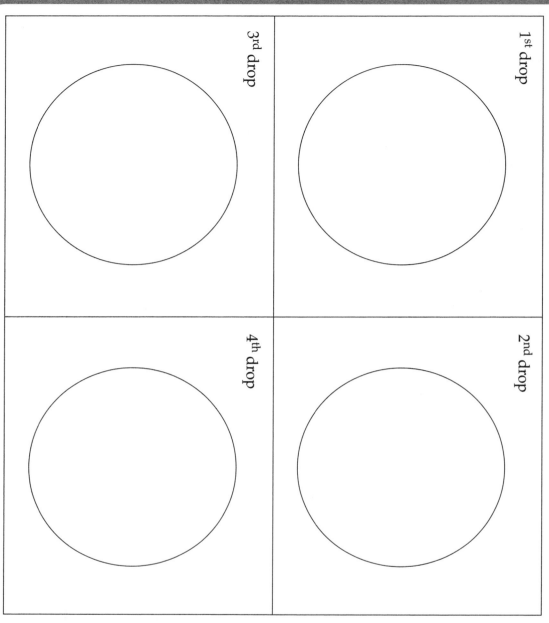

1st drop

2nd drop

3rd drop

4th drop

5 Write your thoughts about this activity.

Dear Teacher:

_____

_____

_____

From,_____
(child's name)

_____
(home partner's name)

6 Get ready for school. Talk about:

- Which game had the most inside the circle?

- What are some combinations we found to make five?

¿Cuántos caen?

Estimada familia:

Nuestra clase está aprendiendo acerca del número cinco.
Jugamos al juego "¿Cuántos caen?" Este juego nos ayudó a aprender a:

- encontrar distintas combinaciones de números que forman cinco
- usar palabras matemáticas como *combinación, igual* y *más*.

En esta actividad, ustedes dos van a jugar a "¿Cuántos caen?"
En clase, conversaremos sobre las combinaciones que encuentren.

❶ Reúnan las cosas que necesiten.

- Cinco frijoles u otros objetos pequeños que no rueden, como macarrones, centavos o botones
- Un lápiz
- El tablero de juego incluido de "¿Cuántos caen?"

❷ Hablen sobre el juego "¿Cuántos caen?" al que jugaron en la escuela.

Cuéntame acerca del juego ¿Cuántos caen? al que jugaron en la escuela.

Dejamos caer cinco cubos sobre un círculo y contamos los que cayeron dentro y fuera del círculo.

❸ Jueguen a "¿Cuántos caen?"

Meta: Contar el número de objetos que caen dentro y fuera del círculo.

- Decidan quién irá primero.
- El primer jugador deja caer los cinco objetos sobre el tablero de juego.

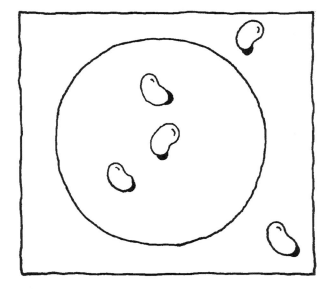

- Juntos, cuenten el número de objetos que cayeron dentro y fuera del círculo.

4 Jueguen a "¿Cuántos caen?" cuatro veces más. Hagan un dibujo o usen números para mostrar cada resultado.

Primer resultado

Segundo resultado

Tercer resultado

Cuarto resultado

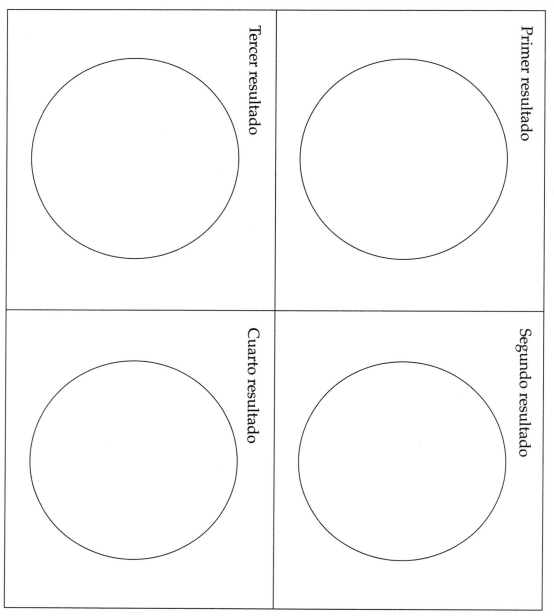

5 Escriban lo que piensan sobre esta actividad.

Estimado maestro:

De, _____
(nombre del niño)

_____
(nombre del compañero en casa)

6 Prepárense para la escuela. Hablen sobre:

- ¿Qué juego tuvo más objetos dentro del círculo?
- ¿Cuáles fueron algunas combinaciones que encontramos que formaban cinco?

Make Five

AT SCHOOL

Pairs play the game "Make Five," finding combinations of beans under cups that make five.

AT HOME

Children teach their home partners to play "Make Five." They record combinations for five.

BACK AT SCHOOL

The class discusses the **At Home** activity and pairs play a guessing game using their **At Home** activities.

Learning About Number

In this activity, children:

- count and compare quantities to five
- explore number combinations for five.

Learning to Work Together

In this activity, children:

- help each other.

Mathematical Vocabulary

group   grupo

combinations

     combinaciones

**"Make Five"
Game Directions**

Goal: Find two groups of beans that total five.

1. Set up the game:

   • Make groups of one to five beans. Cover each group of beans with a cup.

   • Turn over the sixth cup to make a group of zero.

   • Mix up the order of the groups. Move the cups slowly without lifting them, so the beans stay underneath.

2. Decide who will be first.

3. The first player raises one cup and counts the beans.

4. The second player lifts another cup.

5. Together determine if the two groups of beans make five.

6. If the groups make five, remove the beans and the cups. If the groups do not make five, put the cups back over the beans.

7. Continue taking turns until all the beans and cups have been removed.

AT SCHOOL

Get Ready

1. Determine how you will select partners. (See **Forming Pairs,** p. 20.)

2. Prepare materials:

   • A copy of the **At Home** activity, with the return date written on it, for each child

   • Six paper cups or other small opaque containers for each pair

   • Fifteen beans or other small objects of similar size for each pair

Make Connections

1. Select pairs and have partners sit together. First in pairs, then as a class, discuss what children learned about the number five in the previous activity, "Number Drop." Discuss:

Whole Class in Pairs

   (?) **What are some ways to make five?**

   (?) **What are some things you know about the number five?**

   (¿) *¿De qué maneras podemos formar cinco?*

   (¿) *¿Qué cosas saben sobre el número cinco?*

Explain and Model the Game

1. Explain that pairs will play a game about five, called "Make Five."

2. Choose a pair to demonstrate as you explain the game directions one at a time. As the pair models the game, discuss with the class:

   (?) **How many groups can you uncover when it's your turn?**

(?) [Bill's] **first group has** [three] **beans. What group should** [his partner] **try to find to make five? How do you know?**

(?) **How can partners help each other without telling which cup to turn over?**

(?) **Is this a game that someone wins? Why not?**

Teacher Tip
Children can help each other by asking questions. For example, they might ask, "What number do you need to find?" Or "You found the [1] on your last turn. Do you remember where it was?"

(¿) *¿Cuántos grupos pueden destapar cuando es su turno?*

(¿) *El primer grupo de* [Bill] *tiene* [tres] *frijoles. ¿Qué grupo debe destapar* [su compañero] *para formar cinco? ¿Cómo lo saben?*

(¿) *¿Cómo se pueden ayudar los compañeros sin decir la taza que deben levantar?*

(¿) *¿Gana alguien en este juego? ¿Por qué no?*

Pair Work

1. Distribute materials to each pair.

2. Have pairs play the game several times. Circulate and talk with them about the game and their thinking:

Children Working in Pairs

(?) **You've uncovered a group of** [four]. **What group do you need to find? How do you know?**

(?) **What's one way you've found to make five?**

(?) **How are you helping each other?**

(¿) *Han destapado un grupo de* [cuatro], *¿qué grupo necesitan destapar? ¿Cómo lo saben?*

(¿) *¿Cuál es una manera que han encontrado para formar cinco?*

(¿) *¿Cómo se están ayudando?*

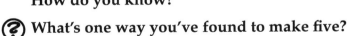

Teacher Tip
Use a strategy such as *Turn to Your Partner* to give all children a chance to think and talk about the questions.

Report and Reflect

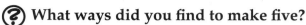
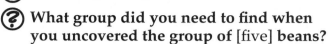
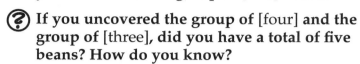
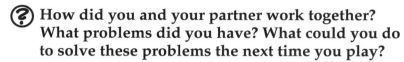

Whole Class in Pairs

1. Discuss the game as a class:

   (?) **What ways did you find to make five?**

   (?) **What group did you need to find when you uncovered the group of [five] beans?**

   (?) **If you uncovered the group of [four] and the group of [three], did you have a total of five beans? How do you know?**

   (?) **How did you and your partner work together? What problems did you have? What could you do to solve these problems the next time you play?**

   (¿) *¿De qué maneras consiguieron formar cinco?*

   (¿) *¿Qué grupo necesitaban encontrar después de destapar el grupo de [cinco] frijoles?*

   (¿) *Si destaparan un grupo de [cuatro] y un grupo de [tres], ¿tendrían un total de cinco frijoles? ¿Cómo lo saben?*

   (¿) *¿Cómo trabajaron juntos tú y tu compañero? ¿Qué problemas tuvieron? ¿Qué pueden hacer para resolver estos problemas la próxima vez que jueguen?*

Prepare for Success at Home

Whole Class

1. Show and explain the **At Home** activity. Explain that children and their home partners will play "Make Five." Ask:

   (?) **What could you use at home to play this game? What else?**

   (¿) *¿Qué pueden usar en casa para jugar a este juego? ¿Qué más?*

2. Explain when children are to bring their **At Home** activity back to class and that their work will be used to play a guessing game.

   (?) **Why is it important for you to do the At Home activity and return it to class?**

   (¿) *¿Por qué es importante hacer y traer a clase la Actividad en casa?*

BACK AT SCHOOL

Get Ready

1. Collect and review the **At Home** activities.

2. Determine how you will select the partners who will work together. Pair children who did not return the **At Home** activity with children who did and have them ask questions about what their partners did at home.

Discuss the At Home Activity

Whole Class in Pairs

Teacher Tip
Use a strategy such as *Think, Pair, Share* to give children time to think on their own before discussing their thinking with others.

1. Select pairs and have partners sit together. Return the **At Home** activities to children. First in pairs, then as a class, discuss:

   (?) Who was your home partner?

   (?) How did you and your home partner help each other?

   (?) What were some ways you found to make five? How do you know this equals five?

   (¿) ¿Quién fue su compañero en casa?

   (¿) ¿Cómo se ayudaron tú y tu compañero en casa a jugar a este juego?

   (¿) ¿De qué maneras consiguieron formar cinco? ¿Cómo supieron que sumaban cinco?

2. Have partners pick one of the "Make Five" games they recorded on their **At Home** activity. Have them take turns covering one of the circles. Ask the other partner to look at the uncovered circle and guess the number in the covered circle. Have partners discuss:

   (?) How did you figure out how many objects were covered? Did anyone do it another way?

   (¿) ¿Cómo averiguaron cuántos objetos cubiertos había? ¿Lo hizo alguien de otra manera?

Extend the Experience

- Play "Make Five," and then have pairs count the total number of beans in the game by putting their beans into groups of five and counting by fives.

- Play "Make Five" and have children keep a written record of all the combinations for five they encounter during the game.

- Provide pairs with beans, glue, and large sheets of construction paper. Have partners glue beans in groups on the paper to show all the ways that they can find to make five. Encourage them to show ways to make five with three, four, and five groups of beans (for example, two beans, two beans, and one bean). As a class, add more combinations of five to the list started in the **Back at School** activity.

- Have children make designs with combinations of five pattern blocks, tiles, or cubes of different colors. Have them record and explain their designs in terms of number sentences: For example, "Two red tiles and three green tiles equal five tiles. 2 + 3 = 5."

- Play "Make Six" and larger numbers.

Make Five

Child's Name:

Return Date:

Dear Family,

Our class is learning about the number five. We played the game "Make Five." This game helped us learn to:

- Make five in different ways, such as four and one, two and three, and five and zero

- use math words such as *group, combinations, less than,* and *more than.*

The two of you will play the game "Make Five." In class, we will use the ways you find to make five to play a game.

① Collect the things you need.

- A pencil, pen, or crayon
- Six cups
- Sixteen beans or other objects of similar size

② Talk about the games that you like to play.

③ Set up the game.

- Make groups of one, two, three, four, and five objects.

- Cover each group of objects with a cup.

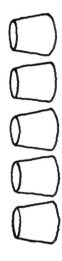

- Turn over the sixth cup with no objects underneath it to make a group of zero.

- Mix up the groups by moving the cups around.

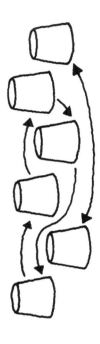

4 Play "Make 5."

The goal is to find two groups of objects that make five.

- Decide who will be first.
- The first player lifts one cup and counts the objects.
- The second player lifts another cup.
- Together, decide if the two groups make five.
- If the groups make five, remove the objects and their cups and put them in a pile.
- If the groups do not make five, put the cups back over the objects.
- Continue taking turns until all the objects are in the pile.

5 Play "Make Five" two more times. Draw or write about the ways you found to make five.

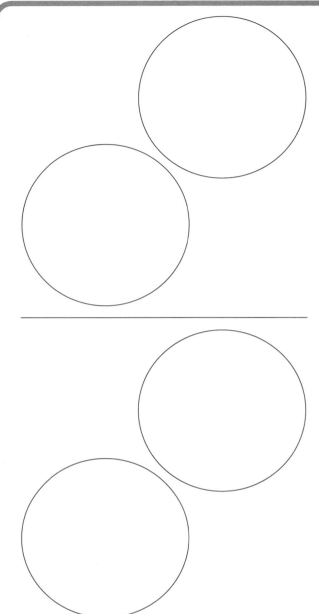

6 Write your thoughts about this activity.

Dear Teacher:

_____

_____

_____

From, _____
         (child's name)

_____
     (home partner's name)

7 Get ready for school.
Talk about:

- What combinations for five did we find for the class chart?
- How can we make sure our **At Home** activity gets back to school?

Formar cinco

Estimada Familia:

Nuestra clase está aprendiendo acerca del número cinco. Jugamos al juego "Formar cinco". Este juego nos ayudó a:

- formar el número cinco de varias maneras como cuatro y uno, dos y tres y cinco y cero.
- usar palabras matemáticas como *grupo, combinaciones, menos que* y *más que.*

Ustedes dos van a jugar al juego de "Formar cinco". En clase, usaremos las maneras en las que formen cinco para jugar a un juego.

❶ Reúnan las cosas que necesiten.

- Un lápiz, una pluma o un creyón
- Seis tazas
- Diez y seis frijoles u otros objetos de tamaño similar

❷ Hablen sobre los juegos a lo que les gusta jugar.

¿A qué juegos jugabas cuando tenías mi edad?

Me encantaba jugar a la rayuela.

¿Qué juegos te gustan a ti?

❸ Preparen el juego.

- Hagan grupos de uno, dos, tres, cuatro y cinco objetos.

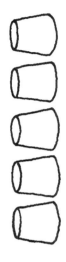

- Tapen cada grupo de objetos con una taza.

- Den la vuelta a la taza número seis sin ningún objeto para hacer un grupo de cero.

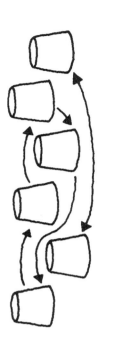

- Mezclen los grupos moviendo las tazas.

4 Jueguen a "Formar cinco".

Meta: Hallar dos grupos de objetos que formen cinco.

- Decidan quién irá primero.
- El primer jugador levanta una taza y cuenta los objetos.
- El segundo jugador levanta otra taza.
- Juntos, decidan si los dos grupos forman cinco.
- Si los grupos forman cinco, retiren los objetos y las tazas y pónganlos en un montón. Si los grupos no forman cinco, tapen de nuevo los objetos con las tazas.
- Continúen turnándose hasta que todos los objetos estén en el montón.

5 Jueguen a "Formar cinco" dos veces más. Dibujen o escriban las maneras en las que consiguieron formar cinco.

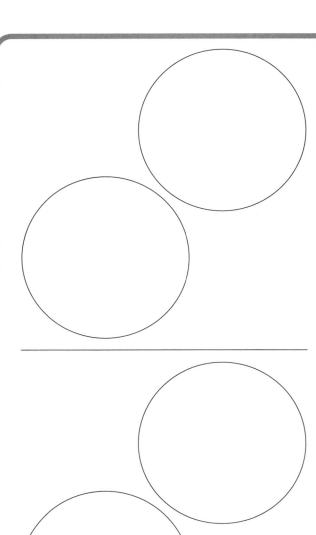

6 Escriban lo que piensan sobre esta actividad.

Estimado maestro:

_____

_____

_____

De, _____

(nombre del niño)

_____

(nombre del compañero en casa)

7 Prepárense para la escuela.
Hablen sobre:

- ¿Qué combinaciones del número cinco encontramos para la tabla de la clase?
- ¿Cómo podemos asegurarnos de traer de vuelta a la escuela la Actividad en casa?

Measurement Activities Overview

MEASUREMENT CONCEPTS

Measurement is an integral part of our lives. During the course of a day we constantly measure as we drive, shop, cook, and schedule our time. Learning to measure has several related components. In kindergarten, instruction focuses on recognizing the attributes to be measured, comparing and ordering objects, choosing an appropriate unit or tool, and understanding how to measure. The three **MathLinks** measurement activities support children's development of these concepts. For children who have had little previous experience measuring, **MathLinks** also includes an introductory activity, on p. 121, that can be explored before the three **MathLinks** activities.

Recognize the Attribute to Be Measured

Young children need to discover that objects have measurable attributes, such as length, capacity, and weight. Some of these attributes, such as length, can be measured directly. Others are measured indirectly, such as temperature, which is measured by determining the height of mercury in a thermometer. The **MathLinks** activities focus on the attribute of length.

Compare and Order Objects

Children develop an understanding of attributes by looking at, touching, or directly comparing objects—for example, putting two objects next to each other to determine which is taller, shorter, longer, or wider. Ordering objects by their attributes and seeing order relationships helps children understand what it means to measure. In "Shorter Than A Straw," children compare the length of objects to the length of a straw and order objects by length. Such measurement is number free, which helps children focus on the attribute being measured.

Choose an Appropriate Unit or Tool

An important aspect of measurement is choosing a unit or tool that is appropriate for the attribute to be measured. Children need experiences choosing and using units for different measuring situations. A straw or paper strip may be an appropriate unit for measuring length, for example, while a square tile or graph paper may be appropriate for measuring area. A paper clip may be more appropriate for measuring the length of a pencil, while a shoe length may be more

appropriate for measuring the length of the classroom. Many experiences measuring with different units and tools will help children discover the inverse relationship between the size of a chosen unit and the number of units required (for example, that covering an area with small units results in a larger number than does covering that same area with large units).

Understand How to Measure

Young children also need to learn about the process of measuring: identifying beginning and ending points of a measurement of length (or of an area to be covered in a measurement of area or of a level considered "filled" in a measurement of capacity); iterating or placing units to avoid overlaps and gaps; and counting units—particularly partial units. Children explore and discuss this process in two of the **MathLinks** activities. In "Stepping Out," children measure the length of objects by walking heel to toe. In "Handy Measurements," they measure objects with their hands.

Learning about Measurement

The following table identifies the specific measurement concepts developed in each of the activities. A solid bullet (●) identifies the main focus of an activity and an open bullet (○) identifies other concepts developed.

	1. Shorter than a Straw	2. Stepping Out	3. Handy Measurements
Make predictions	●		
Use direct comparison to measure	●		
Compare and order objects by length	●		
Identify beginning and ending points	●	●	●
Use non-standard units to measure		●	●
Repeat a unit to measure		●	●
Use mathematical language	●	●	●

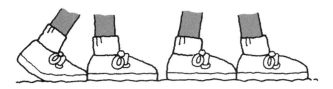

WORKING TOGETHER

In the **MathLinks** activities, children work with partners at school and at home. The goal is to enhance their mathematical development while at the same time helping them learn to work together successfully, communicate effectively, and be responsible learners.

Work with Others

Most kindergarten children are ready to begin to work with a partner. The **MathLinks** measurement activities help children develop initial group skills such as sharing the work, helping each other, and making decisions together.

Communicate Thinking

In addition to frequent opportunities to discuss their thinking and exchange points of view, in the **MathLinks** measurement activities, children record and discuss their results, which helps them learn to organize and communicate mathematical ideas.

Be Responsible

Helping children learn to be responsible means giving them opportunities to assume responsibility and helping them acquire strategies to do so successfully. Children's understanding of what it means to be responsible and how to be responsible develops over time, with many experiences, and with opportunities to talk about them. **MathLinks** helps children be responsible for

- their learning and behavior in school and at home

- getting the home activities to and from home

- finding a home partner and completing the activities

- at times, teaching something to a home partner

- explaining to others what they did at school and at home.

Learning to Work Together

The following table identifies the social skills focus of each activity. A solid bullet (●) identifies the main focus, and an open bullet (○) identifies other skills children might practice.

	1. Shorter then a Straw	2. Stepping Out	3. Handy Measurements
Share the work	●	○	●
Make decisions together	●	●	●
Help each other	○	●	○

MEASUREMENT ACTIVITIES AT A GLANCE

1. Shorter Than a Straw

Pairs predict the objects in the classroom that may be shorter than a straw and then compare them to the straw. They record their findings on a class chart and talk about them with the class. Children and their home partners also make predictions and find objects that are shorter than the straw. They record their results and pick one of the objects to go to school. Back at school, pairs discuss, compare, and order the objects.

2. Stepping Out

Pairs measure the length of objects by walking heel to toe. They then record the measurements on a chart that is discussed by the class. Children and their home partners also measure objects by walking heel to toe and record their results. Back at school, pairs discuss their results from home.

3. Handy Measurements

Pairs use their hands to measure the length of objects, then record and discuss their measurements. Children and their

home partners do the same. Back at school, pairs discuss their results from home. A child and the teacher measure the length of the same object with their hands and compare the results.

LITERATURE LINKS

***The Long and Short of It* by Cheryl Nathan and Lisa McCourt** (Bridgewater Paperback/Troll, 1999). This imaginative book compares animals to every day objects, making comparisons such as, a raccoon's "tongue is as short as a stick of gum" and a crocodile's "grin is longer than your pillow." Consider using this book to introduce the terms *longer* and *shorter* before beginning the activity "Shorter Than a Straw."

***How Big Is a Foot?* by Rolf Myller** (Dell Publishing, 1991). In this tale, a king commands a carpenter's apprentice to make a bed for the queen. When the apprentice asks what size the bed should be, the king declares that it should be six feet long and three feet wide. Why, then, when it is built to the king's measurements, is the bed too small for the queen? Fortunately, the clever apprentice solves the problem. In doing so, he is saved from jail and proclaimed a prince. This book can be used to introduce children to the idea of measuring with footsteps before the class begins the activity, "Stepping Out."

***Inch by Inch* by Leo Lionni** (Scholastic Inc., 1995). In this book, an inchworm convinces a hungry robin not to eat him by saying that he is useful because he can measure things. Consider using this book before the class begins the activity "Handy Measurements" to discuss the body as a measurement tool

Pulgada a pulgada by Leo Lionni
(Scholastic Inc., 1995) The Spanish version of *Inch by Inch* (see description above). Although currently out of print, copies are available in libraries.

KINDERGARTEN MEASUREMENT INTRODUCTORY ACTIVITY

If children have not had previous experience with such initial measuring concepts as identifying attributes of objects, directly comparing the lengths of objects, or ordering objects by length, introduce an activity such as the following before exploring the **MathLinks** activities.

1. Put three shoes of various sizes in a bag. Use very different shoes (such as a large sneaker, a smaller sandal, and a baby shoe) to make it easier for children to discuss each shoe's individual attributes as well as their similarities and differences. [Note: You may want to clean or otherwise disinfect the shoes before this activity.]

2. Begin by saying, **I wonder if you can guess what's in my bag. Each of us has some of these but they could be different in some way.**

   (?) **What do you think I might have in my bag?**

3. Take a shoe from the bag and place it where everyone can see it. Discuss:

   (?) **What do you notice about this shoe?**

   (?) **How is this shoe like the shoe you are wearing? How is it different?**

   (?) **What other kinds of shoes do you think might be in my bag?**

4. Take another shoe from the bag. First in pairs, then as a class, discuss:

   (?) **What do you notice about this shoe?**

   (?) **How is this shoe like the first shoe? How is it different?**

   (?) **How is this shoe like the shoe you are wearing? How is it different?**

   (?) **Which of these two shoes is longer? How do you know?**

   (?) **Who can put these shoes in order by how long they are? Show us. Is there another way to order them by how long they are? Show us.**

   (?) **I have one more shoe in my bag. How do you think it might look?**

5. Take the third shoe from the bag. First in pairs, then as a class, discuss:

   (?) **What do you notice about this shoe?**

   (?) **How is this shoe like the other two shoes? How is it different?**

   (?) **How is this shoe like the shoe you are wearing? How is it different?**

? Which of these three shoes is longest? How do you know?

? Which is shortest? How do you know?

? How could we put these three shoes in order by how long they are? Who would like to show us? Why do you think that works? Is there another way to put them in order by how long they are? Show us. Why do you think that works?

Shorter Than a Straw

AT SCHOOL

In pairs, children predict the objects in the classroom that may be shorter than a straw and then compare them to the straw. Pairs record their findings on a class chart and discuss the results with the class.

AT HOME

Children and their home partners make predictions about the objects in their home that may be shorter than a straw. They compare them to the straw, record their results, and pick one of the objects to go to school.

BACK AT SCHOOL

In pairs, children discuss, compare, and order the objects they brought from home.

Learning About Measurement

In this activity, children:

- make predictions
- use direct comparisons to measure
- compare and order objects by length
- identify beginning and ending points.

Learning to Work Together

In this activity, the children:

- share the work
- make decisions together.

Mathematical Vocabulary

measure	medir
predict	predecir
shorter	más corto que
longer	más largo que
order	poner en orden
compare	comparar

AT SCHOOL

Get Ready

1. If children have had little experience with initial measurement concepts, provide an experience such as the introductory activity suggested in the "Measurement Activities Overview," pp.117–122.

2. Determine how you will select partners. (See **Forming Pairs,** p. 20.)

3. Prepare materials:

   - A copy of the Measurement Activities Family Letter, p. 15, for each child (You may want to attach it to the **At Home** activity.)

   - A copy of the **At Home** activity, with the return date written on it, for each child.

   - A straw for each child, attached to the **At Home** activity. All straws should be the same length.

   - A straw for each pair. All straws should be the same length.

   - A pencil and a sticky note for each pair

   - A chart labeled "Objects Shorter Than a Straw"

Literature Link

The Long and Short of It by Cheryl Nathan and Lisa McCourt (Bridgewater Paperback/Troll, 1999). Introduce the activity with this book to help children understand the terms longer and shorter. (optional)

Make Connections

1. Select pairs and have partners sit together. Introduce and discuss the term *measure*.

   Whole Class in Pairs

   (?) **What do you think the word *measure* means?**

   (?) **When have you measured something?**

   (?) **When have you seen someone measure?**

   (?) **Have you ever been measured at the doctor's office? Why do doctors measure how tall you are? What do doctors use to measure how tall you are?**

   (¿) *¿Qué piensan que quiere decir la palabra* medir*?*

   (¿) *¿Cuándo han medido algo?*

(¿) *¿Cuándo han visto a alguien medir algo?*

(¿) *¿Los han medido alguna vez en la consulta del médico? ¿Por qué los miden los médicos? ¿Qué usan los médicos para medir su altura?*

2. Show a straw to the class. Ask whether children think that the straw is long or short and why they think so.

3. Wonder aloud, "What things in our classroom might be shorter than the straw?" Have children look around the room and name some objects that they predict are shorter than the straw. Discuss:

   (?) **How could you find out if that is shorter than a straw?**

   (¿) *¿Cómo pueden averiguar si eso es más corto que una pajita?*

Explain and Model the Activity

1. Choose a child to demonstrate the activity with you. As you model, discuss:

   (?) **How can we decide on an object to measure? Is that fair? What can we do if we don't agree?**

   (?) **Is this an object that we can easily take back to our places to share with others? If not, what might we do?** (Help children recognize that some objects such as those that are heavy or breakable are not appropriate objects to share.)

   (?) **How can we find out if the object we chose is shorter than our straw?**

   (?) **How can we work together to write on the sticky note and put the it on the chart? Is that fair?**

   (¿) *¿Cómo podemos decidir qué objeto medir? ¿Es eso justo? ¿Qué podemos hacer si no estamos de acuerdo?*

   (¿) *¿Es éste un objeto que podemos llevar fácilmente a la alfombra para compartir con los demás? Si no, ¿qué podemos hacer?* (Ayude a los niños a reconocer que algunos objetos, como los pesados o los que se rompen fácilmente, no son objetos apropiados para compartir).

Activity Directions
Pairs:

• predict which objects in the classroom may be shorter than the straw. Find an object that is shorter than the straw

• draw that object and write their names on the sticky note

• place the sticky note on the chart labeled, "Objects Shorter Than a Straw"

• bring the object back to their places for a class discussion.

Teacher Tip
If it doesn't come up naturally, suggest lining up the beginning points of the straw and an object to compare their lengths.

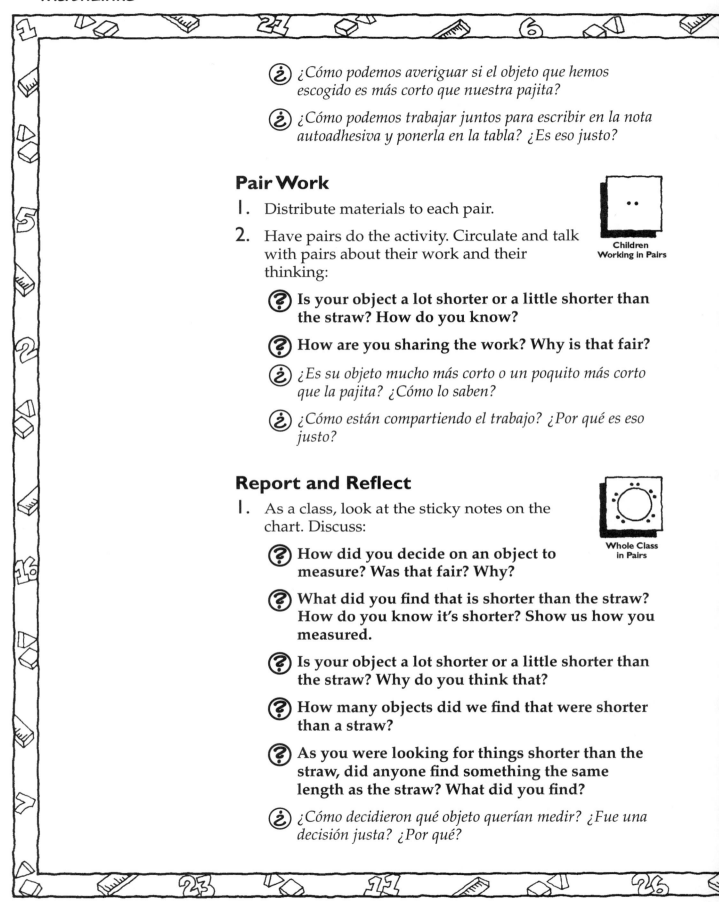

¿ ¿Cómo podemos averiguar si el objeto que hemos escogido es más corto que nuestra pajita?

¿ ¿Cómo podemos trabajar juntos para escribir en la nota autoadhesiva y ponerla en la tabla? ¿Es eso justo?

Pair Work

1. Distribute materials to each pair.

2. Have pairs do the activity. Circulate and talk with pairs about their work and their thinking:

Children Working in Pairs

? **Is your object a lot shorter or a little shorter than the straw? How do you know?**

? **How are you sharing the work? Why is that fair?**

¿ *¿Es su objeto mucho más corto o un poquito más corto que la pajita? ¿Cómo lo saben?*

¿ *¿Cómo están compartiendo el trabajo? ¿Por qué es eso justo?*

Report and Reflect

1. As a class, look at the sticky notes on the chart. Discuss:

Whole Class in Pairs

? **How did you decide on an object to measure? Was that fair? Why?**

? **What did you find that is shorter than the straw? How do you know it's shorter? Show us how you measured.**

? **Is your object a lot shorter or a little shorter than the straw? Why do you think that?**

? **How many objects did we find that were shorter than a straw?**

? **As you were looking for things shorter than the straw, did anyone find something the same length as the straw? What did you find?**

¿ *¿Cómo decidieron qué objeto querían medir? ¿Fue una decisión justa? ¿Por qué?*

(¿) *¿Qué encontraron que es más corto que la pajita?*
¿Cómo saben que es más corto? Muéstrennos cómo
midieron.

(¿) *¿Es su objeto mucho más corto o un poquito más corto*
que la pajita? ¿Por qué piensan eso?

(¿) *¿Cuántos objetos encontramos que eran más cortos que*
una pajita?

(¿) *Mientras buscaban cosas más cortas que una pajita,*
¿encontró alguien algo igual de largo que la pajita?
¿Qué encontraron?

Prepare for Success at Home

1. Show and explain the **At Home** activity.
    Explain that children and their home partners
    will find and draw objects that are shorter
    than a straw and that children will bring one
    of their objects to class. Show the straw
    attached to the **At Home** activity. Ask:

    Whole Class

    (?) **Who might you ask to be your home partner?**
    What will you do if that person is busy?

    (?) **What do you think that you have at home that**
    might be shorter than the straw?

    (¿) *¿A quién podrían pedir que fuese su compañero en*
    casa? ¿Qué harán si esa persona está ocupada?

    (¿) *¿Qué piensan que tienen en casa que podría ser más*
    corto que la pajita?

2. Explain when children are to bring their **At Home**
    activities back to class and that the class will discuss
    and compare the objects they bring from home.
    Talk about the types of objects children might bring to
    school (things that are not valuable, sharp, breakable,
    or heavy). Explain that children and their home part-
    ners should decide on the objects together and label the
    objects with their names.

BACK AT SCHOOL

Get Ready

1. Collect and review the **At Home** activities and the objects the children brought from home. Be sure all objects are labeled with a child's name.

2. Determine how you will select partners.

Discuss the At Home Activity

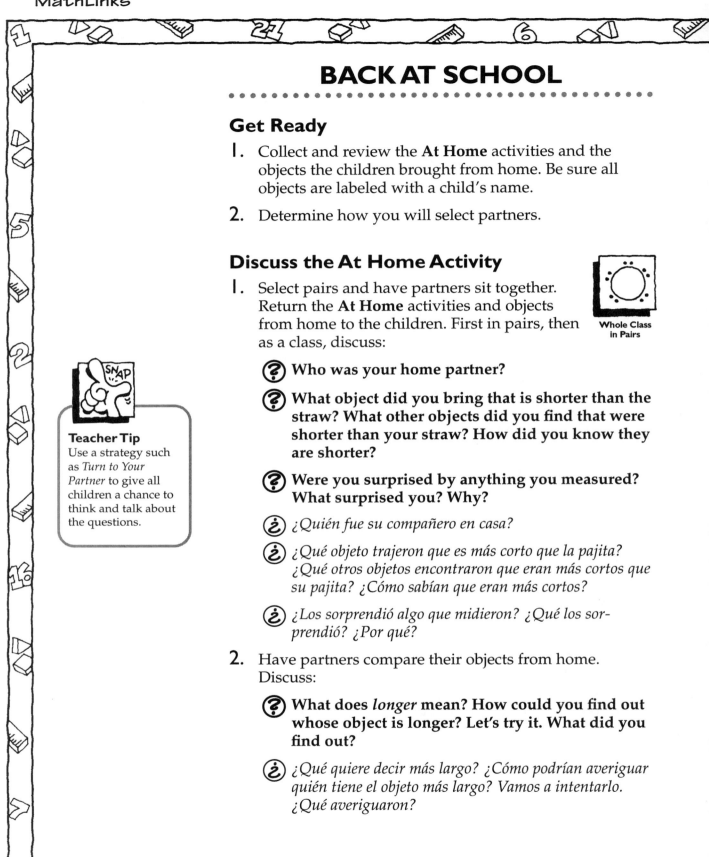

Whole Class in Pairs

1. Select pairs and have partners sit together. Return the **At Home** activities and objects from home to the children. First in pairs, then as a class, discuss:

   ? Who was your home partner?

   ? What object did you bring that is shorter than the straw? What other objects did you find that were shorter than your straw? How did you know they are shorter?

   ? Were you surprised by anything you measured? What surprised you? Why?

   ¿ ¿Quién fue su compañero en casa?

   ¿ ¿Qué objeto trajeron que es más corto que la pajita? ¿Qué otros objetos encontraron que eran más cortos que su pajita? ¿Cómo sabían que eran más cortos?

   ¿ ¿Los sorprendió algo que midieron? ¿Qué los sorprendió? ¿Por qué?

2. Have partners compare their objects from home. Discuss:

   ? What does *longer* mean? How could you find out whose object is longer? Let's try it. What did you find out?

   ¿ ¿Qué quiere decir más largo? ¿Cómo podrían averiguar quién tiene el objeto más largo? Vamos a intentarlo. ¿Qué averiguaron?

Teacher Tip
Use a strategy such as *Turn to Your Partner* to give all children a chance to think and talk about the questions.

Extend the Experience

- As a class, order all of the objects from home by length.

- Have pairs find, record, and discuss objects in the classroom that are longer or the same length as a straw.

- Have pairs find, record, and discuss objects that are longer, shorter, or the same length as a pencil or other object.

Shorter Than a Straw

Dear Family,

Our class is learning about measurement. We found and discussed objects that are shorter than a straw. This helped us learn to:

- measure length by comparing objects
- use math words such as *measure, compare,* and *shorter.*

In this activity, the two of you will find objects that are shorter than a straw and choose one to send back to school. In class, we will compare and order the length of the objects.

① Collect the things you need.
- A pencil, pen, or crayon
- The attached straw

② Talk about when and why you measure things.

When do you measure?

When I move furniture in a room, I measure to see where each piece will fit.

③ Do the activity.

- Look for objects in your home that might be shorter than the straw.
- When you find something, compare it to the straw to find out which is shorter.

Talk about:
- What did we find that is shorter than a straw?
- How do we know that it is shorter than the straw?

4 Draw pictures of the objects you find that are shorter than the straw.

5 Write your thoughts about this activity.

Dear Teacher:

_____

_____

_____

From, _____
(child's name)

_____
(home partner's name)

6 Get ready for school.

• Decide which one of the objects can be taken to school. Label it with the child's name. (The object should not be heavy, sharp, breakable, or valuable.)

Talk about:

• How will you remember to take the object we've chosen to school?

Más corto que una pajita

Estimada familia:

Nuestra clase está aprendiendo acerca de las medidas. Encontramos y conversamos acerca de los objetos que eran más cortos que una pajita. Esto nos ayudó a aprender a:

- medir longitud comparando objetos
- usar palabras matemáticas como *medir, comparar y más corto*.

En esta actividad, ustedes dos buscarán objetos que sean más cortos que una pajita y escogerán uno para mandar a la escuela. En clase, compararemos y pondremos los objetos en orden según su longitud.

① Reúnan las cosas que necesiten.
- Un lápiz, una pluma o un creyón
- La pajita incluida

② Hablen sobre cuándo y por qué miden cosas.

¿Cuándo mides?

Cuando muevo muebles dentro de una habitación, mido para ver dónde va a caber cada pieza.

③ Hagan la actividad.

- Busquen objetos en su casa que podrían ser más cortos que la pajita incluida.
- Cuando encuentren algo, compárenlo con la pajita para averiguar cuál es más corto.

Hablen sobre:
- ¿Qué encontramos que es más corto que una pajita?
  ¿Cómo sabemos que es más corto que una pajita?

4 Hagan dibujos de los objetos que encuentren que sean más cortos que la pajita.

5 Escriban lo que piensan sobre esta actividad.

Estimado maestro:

_____

_____

De, _____

(nombre del niño)

_____

(nombre del compañero en casa)

6 **Prepárense para la escuela.**

• Decidan cuál de los objetos se puede llevar a la escuela. Escriban el nombre del niño en el objeto. (El objeto no debe ser pesado, afilado, fácil de romper o valioso.)

Hablen sobre:

• ¿Cómo recordarás que tienes que llevar a la escuela el objeto que escogimos?

Stepping Out

AT SCHOOL

In pairs, children measure the length of objects by walking heel to toe. They record and place them on a chart. The class discusses the data on the chart.

AT HOME

Children and their home partners measure the length of two objects by walking heel to toe. They record and discuss the measurements.

BACK AT SCHOOL

Pairs discuss their results from home.

Learning About Measurement

In this activity, the children:

- identify beginning and ending points of a measurement
- use nonstandard units to measure
- repeat a unit to measure.

Learning to Work Together

In this activity, the children:

- make decisions together
- help each other.

Mathematical Vocabulary

length	longitud
height	altura
a little more [less]	un poco más [menos]
almost	casi

AT SCHOOL

Literature Link
How Big Is a Foot?
by Rolf Myller (Dell
Publishing, 1991).
Introduce the
activity with this
book to help children
understand how to
measure with
footsteps. (optional)

Teacher Tip
Some ancient
civilizations created
measurement
systems based on the
length and width of
certain parts of the
body. For example,
the inch was derived
from the ancient
Roman unit called
the uncia, based on
the width of a
thumb. Twelve uncia
equaled a foot, the
approximate length
of a man's foot.

Get Ready

1. Determine how you will select partners. (See **Forming Pairs,** p. 20.)

2. Prepare materials:

   • A copy of the **At Home** activity, with the return date written on it, for each child

   • A pencil and a sticky note for each pair

   • A large chalkboard, whiteboard, or piece of chart paper

   • A piece of chalk or a few colored marking pens for the teacher

Make Connections

1. Select pairs and have partners sit together. Explain that long ago people measured by using parts of their bodies, such as fingers, hands, arms, and feet. Point out that even today, a horse's height is measured in hands.

Whole Class in Pairs

2. Explain that in this activity, children will use their feet to measure objects in the classroom. Ask:

   (?) **Imagine using your feet to measure the length of the** [bookshelf]. **How would you do it? What is another way?**

   (¿) *Imaginen que pueden usar sus pies para medir la longitud* [del estante]. *¿Cómo lo harían? ¿Hay alguna otra manera de hacerlo?*

3. If no one suggests measuring by walking heel to toe, suggest this method and ask for a volunteer to help you demonstrate. Help the volunteer walk so that each heel touches the toe of the other shoe. Have everyone practice walking heel to toe.

4. As a class, choose five to eight objects large enough to measure by walking heel to toe. When the class agrees on an object, draw and label it on the chalkboard, whiteboard, or piece of chart paper.

Explain and Model the Activity

1. Choose a child to demonstrate the activity with you. As you model, discuss with your partner:

(?) **How will we decide what to measure? How will we decide who will measure it and who will count and record? Is that fair? Why or why not?**

(?) **Where should I place my foot to begin to measure this [bookcase]? Where should I stop?**

(¿) *¿Cómo decidiremos qué vamos a medir? ¿Cómo decidiremos quién lo medirá y quién contará y anotará los resultados? ¿Es eso justo? ¿Por qué?*

(¿) *¿Dónde debo poner mi pie para empezar a medir este [estante]? ¿Dónde debo parar?*

2. Discuss with the class:

(?) **What could you do if another pair is measuring the object you've chosen?**

(¿) *¿Qué pueden hacer si otra pareja de estudiantes está midiendo el objeto que ustedes han escogido?*

Pair Work

1. Distribute materials to each pair.

2. Have pairs do the activity. Circulate and talk with pairs about their work and their thinking:

(?) **How are you helping each other do this activity?**

(?) **How many of [Ashaki's] steps did it take to measure the [jump rope]? Where did you start measuring? Where did you stop?**

(¿) *¿Cómo se están ayudando para hacer esta actividad?*

(¿) *¿Cuántos pasos dio [Ashaki] para medir la cuerda de saltar? ¿Dónde empezaron a medir? ¿Dónde pararon?*

3. Ask pairs who finish early to measure other objects in the room.

Children Working in Pairs

Activity Directions:
Pairs:

- choose an object from the chart to measure

- decide who will measure the object by walking heel to toe and who will count and record the number of steps on the sticky note

- measure and record the number of steps

- place the sticky note on the chart next to the picture of the object.

Teacher Tip
Encourage children to choose objects that they can measure directly with the heel-to-toe method. For example, children can place their feet next to the base of a bookcase but can not place them next to a tabletop. Other objects that work well are those that can be placed flat on the floor, such as a jump rope or a bin.

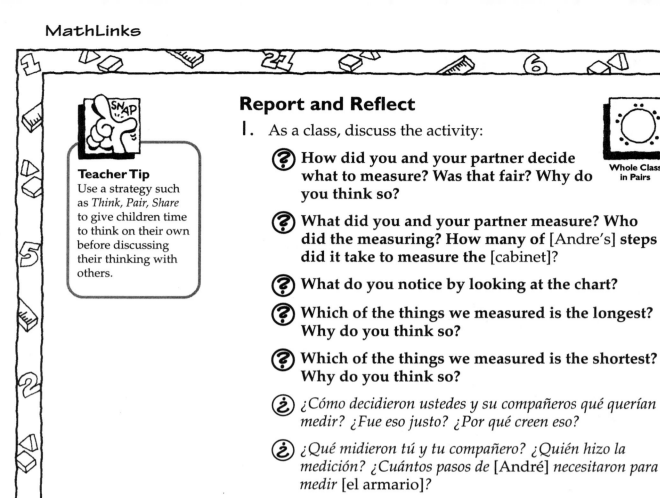

Teacher Tip
Use a strategy such as *Think, Pair, Share* to give children time to think on their own before discussing their thinking with others.

Report and Reflect

1. As a class, discuss the activity:

Whole Class in Pairs

(?) **How did you and your partner decide what to measure? Was that fair? Why do you think so?**

(?) **What did you and your partner measure? Who did the measuring? How many of** [Andre's] **steps did it take to measure the** [cabinet]**?**

(?) **What do you notice by looking at the chart?**

(?) **Which of the things we measured is the longest? Why do you think so?**

(?) **Which of the things we measured is the shortest? Why do you think so?**

(¿) *¿Cómo decidieron ustedes y su compañeros qué querían medir? ¿Fue eso justo? ¿Por qué creen eso?*

(¿) *¿Qué midieron tú y tu compañero? ¿Quién hizo la medición? ¿Cuántos pasos de* [André] *necesitaron para medir* [el armario]*?*

(¿) *¿Qué notan al mirar la tabla?*

(¿) *De las cosas que medimos, ¿cuál es la más larga? ¿Por qué creen eso?*

(¿) *De las cosas que medimos, ¿cuál es la más corta? ¿Por qué creen eso?*

Prepare for Success at Home

1. Show and explain the **At Home** activity. Explain that children and their home partners will measure and record the number of each of their steps it takes to measure two objects. Ask:

Whole Class

(?) **What will you and your home partner do? What might you measure?**

(?) **How can you and your home partner help each other do this activity?**

(¿) *¿Qué van a hacer tú y tu compañero en casa? ¿Qué van a medir?*

(**¿**) *¿Cómo pueden ayudarse para hacer esta actividad?*

2. Explain when children are to bring their **At Home** activities back to class and that the class will discuss the measurements they make at home.

> (**?**) **When do we need to have the At Home activities back at school?**

> (**¿**) *¿Cuándo necesitamos traer a la escuela las Actividades en casa?*

BACK AT SCHOOL

Get Ready

1. Collect and review **At Home** activities.

2. Determine how you will select the partners.

Discuss the At Home Activity

1. Select pairs and have partners sit together. Return the **At Home** activities to children. First in pairs, then as a class, discuss:

Whole Class in Pairs

> (**?**) **What objects did you and your home partner measure?**

> (**?**) **What did you find out?**

> (**?**) **Which of the two objects you measured at home was shorter? How do you know?**

> (**?**) **How many child's steps long did your first object measure? How many home partner's steps long did your first object measure? Why are the numbers different?**

> (**¿**) *¿Qué objetos midieron tú y tu compañero en casa?*

> (**¿**) *¿Qué averiguaron?*

> (**¿**) *¿Cuál de los dos objetos que midieron en casa era más corto? ¿Cómo lo saben?*

Teacher Tip
Choose a strategy such as *Pair Q and A* to help children learn to ask a partner questions.

¿ *¿Cuántos pasos de niño midió su primer objeto? ¿Cuántos pasos de su compañero en casa midió el primer objeto? ¿Por qué son los números diferentes?*

Extend the Experience

- Have the class choose an object that can be measured heel to toe and place it in a center. Invite special guests such as the principal or custodian to visit your room to measure the object by stepping heel to toe. Record, discuss, and compare the visitors' measurements.

- Have pairs use footsteps to measure distances in the classroom such as from the doorway to the easel.

Stepping Out

Dear Family,

Our class is learning about measurement. We measured objects in the classroom by walking heel to toe. This helped us learn to:

- measure length using units (a footstep)
- use math words such as *measure, a little more,* and *a little less.*

In this activity, the two of you will choose two objects to measure. You will measure their lengths by walking heel to toe and write about what you find. In class, we will discuss your measurements.

❸ Do the activity.

- Help each other practice walking heel to toe. Touch the heel of one shoe to the toe of the other and count each step aloud.

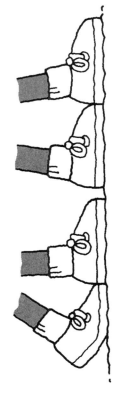

- Walk around your home and find an object to measure.
- Measure the object by walking heel to toe and counting the number of steps each partner takes.

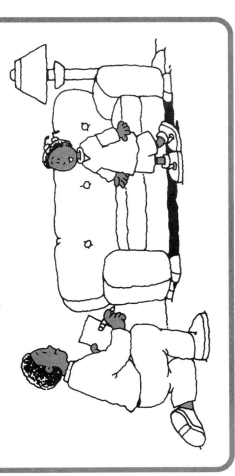

❶ Collect the things you need.
- A pencil, pen, or crayon

❷ Talk about a time when you measured something by walking heel to toe (or in another way).

Have you ever measured something by walking heel to toe?

Yes, I measured the sofa to see if it would fit against the back wall.

4 **Draw a picture of the object and write its length in child's steps and in home partner's steps.**

First Object:

Child's steps ———   Home Partner's steps ———

5 **Do this again with a different object.**

Second Object:

Child's steps ———   Home Partner's steps ———

6 **Write your thoughts about this activity.**

Dear Teacher:

_____

_____

_____

From,

_____
(child's name)

_____
(home partner's name)

7 **Get ready for school. Talk about:**

• Did it take more of my steps or your steps to measure the object? Why do you think that happened?

• Which of our objects is shorter? Which is longer? Why do you think so?

Dar un paso

Estimada familia:

Nuestra clase está aprendiendo acerca de las medidas. Medimos objetos en la clase caminando de talón a punta. Esto nos ayudó a aprender a:

- medir longitud usando unidades (un paso)
- usar palabras matemáticas como, *un poco más, un poco menos* y *casi.*

En esta actividad, ambos escogerán dos objetos para medir. Medirán sus longitudes caminando de talón a punta y escribirán sobre lo que averigüen. En clase, comentaremos sus medidas.

❶ Reúnan las cosas que necesiten.

- Un lápiz, una pluma o un creyón

❷ Hablen sobre una vez en que midieron algo caminando de talón a punta (o de otra manera).

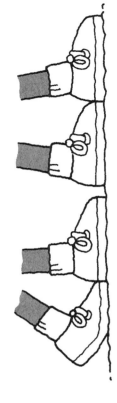

¿Has medido algo caminando de punta a talón?

Sí. Medí el sofá ver si cabía contra la pared de atrás.

❸ Hagan la actividad.

- Ayúdense el uno al otro a practicar caminando de talón a punta. Toquen el talón de uno de los zapatos con la punta del otro y cuenten cada paso en voz alta.

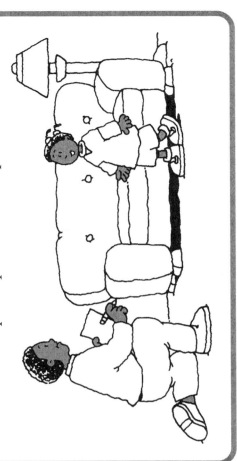

- Caminen por la casa y busquen un objeto para medir.
- Midan el objeto caminando de talón a punta y contando el número de pasos que da cada compañero.

4 Hagan un dibujo del objeto y escriban su longitud en pasos de niño y en pasos del compañero en casa.

Primer objeto:

Pasos del niño _____   Pasos del compañero en casa _____

5 Háganlo de nuevo con un objeto distinto.

Segundo objeto:

Pasos del niño _____   Pasos del compañero en casa _____

5 Escriban lo que piensan sobre esta actividad.

Estimado maestro:

_____

_____

_____

De, _____

(nombre del niño)

_____

(nombre del compañero en casa)

7 Prepárense para la escuela. Hablen sobre:

- ¿Necesitamos más pasos míos o más pasos tuyos para medir el objeto? ¿Por qué piensas que pasó eso?
- ¿Cuál de nuestros objetos es más corto? ¿Cuál es más largo? ¿Por qué piensas eso?

Handy Measurements

AT SCHOOL

In pairs, children use their hands to measure the length of objects. They record and discuss their measurements.

AT HOME

Children and their home partners use their hands to measure the length of two objects. They record and discuss the measurements.

BACK AT SCHOOL

In pairs, children discuss their results from home. Then a child and the teacher measure the length of the same object with their hands and compare the results.

Learning About Measurement

In this activity, the children:

- identify beginning and ending points of a measurement
- use nonstandard units to measure
- repeat a unit to measure.

Learning to Work Together

In this activity, the children:

- share the work
- make decisions together.

Mathematical Vocabulary

length   longitud

AT SCHOOL

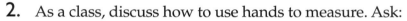

Get Ready

1. Determine how you will select partners. (See **Forming Pairs**, p. 20.)

2. Prepare materials:

   • A copy of the **At Home** activity, with the return date written on it, for each child

   • A pencil and a sheet of paper

Make Connections

1. Select pairs and have partners sit together. Review the previous activity, "Stepping Out." Explain that in "Stepping Out" children measured objects with their feet, and that in this activity, children will use their hands to measure objects in the classroom.

Whole Class in Pairs

2. As a class, discuss how to use hands to measure. Ask:

   (?) **Why is it important to leave no spaces between your hands when measuring?**

   (?) **How do you know where to start measuring? Where to stop measuring?**

   (¿) *¿Por qué es importante no dejar espacios entre sus manos cuando están midiendo?*

   (¿) *¿Cómo saben dónde deben empezar a medir? ¿Dónde deben parar de medir?*

Activity Directions

Pairs:

• choose an object to measure and draw the object on their paper

• decide who will measure and who will count and record the number of hands

• measure and record the number of hands

• switch roles and measure a different object.

Explain and Model the Activity

1. Choose a volunteer to demonstrate the activity with you. As you model, discuss with the class:

   (?) **What's a way my partner and I can decide what to measure? How could we decide who will measure and who will count and record?**

   (?) **About how many of [Kevin's] hands do you think it will take to measure this [table]?**

(¿) *¿De qué manera podemos decidir mi compañero y yo qué medir? ¿Cómo podemos decidir quién va a medir y quién va a contar y anotar las medidas?*

(¿) *¿Cuántas manos de [Kevin] creen que necesitamos para medir esta [mesa]?*

Pair Work

Children Working in Pairs

1. Distribute materials to each pair.

2. Have pairs do the activity. Circulate and talk with them about their work and their thinking:

   (?) **I notice that your last hand goes beyond the [table]? How many hands long is your measurement?**

   (?) **I see by what you've recorded that you measured a bookcase and it is [seven] hands long. Whose hands did you use? Show me how you measured.**

   (¿) *Veo que su última mano pasa más allá de [la mesa]. ¿Cuántas manos de largo tiene su medida?*

   (¿) *Veo en sus notas que midieron un estante y que tiene [siete] manos de largo. ¿Qué manos usaron? Muéstrenme cómo midieron.*

3. Ask pairs that finish early to measure other objects in the room.

Report and Reflect

Whole Class in Pairs

1. As a class, discuss the activity:

   (?) **How did you decide what to measure? Was that fair? Why do you think so?**

   (?) **What objects did you measure? What did you find out? How many of [Cassandra's] hands did it take to measure the [desk]?**

   (?) **Which of the objects that you measured is [longer]? Why do you think that?**

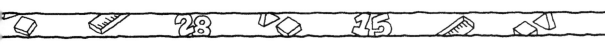

¿ *¿Cómo decidieron qué medir? ¿Fue justo? ¿Por qué creen eso?*

¿ *¿Qué objetos midieron? ¿Qué averiguaron? ¿Cuántas manos de [Cassandra] necesitaron para medir [el escritorio]?*

¿ *¿Cuál de los objetos que midieron es más largo? ¿Por qué creen eso?*

Prepare for Success at Home

1. Show and explain the **At Home** activity. Explain that children and their home partners will measure and record the number of each of their hands it takes to measure two objects. Ask:

   ? **What are some objects at home that you could measure with your hands?**

   ? **How can you and your home partner help each other measure?**

   ¿ *¿Cuáles son algunos de los objetos que podrían medir en casa con sus manos?*

   ¿ *¿Cómo pueden ayudarse ustedes y sus compañeros en casa para medir?*

2. Explain when children are to bring their **At Home** activities back to class and that the class will discuss the measurements they make at home.

   ? **What might help you remember to bring the At Home activity to school?**

   ¿ *¿Qué les ayudaría a recordar que tienen que traer a la escuela su Actividad en casa?*

BACK AT SCHOOL

Get Ready

1. Collect and review **At Home** activities.

2. Determine how you will select partners.

3. Prepare materials:

   • A chalkboard, whiteboard, or piece of chart paper

   • Chalk or colored marking pens for the teacher

Discuss the At Home Activity

1. Select pairs and have partners sit together. Return the **At Home** activities to children. First in pairs, then as a class, discuss:

   Whole Class in Pairs

   (?) **What did you and your home partner measure? When would it be useful to measure the** [sofa]?

   (?) **Did it take more of your hands or more of your home partner's hands to measure the** [sofa]? **Why do you think this happened?**

   (?) **Which of the two things you measured at home was longer? How do you know?**

   (¿) *¿Qué midieron ustedes y sus compañeros en casa? ¿Cuándo sería útil medir* [el sofá]?

   (¿) *¿Necesitaron más manos suyas o más manos de sus compañeros en casa para medir* [el sofá]? *¿Por qué creen que pasó esto?*

   (¿) *¿Cuál de las cosas que midieron en casa era la más larga? ¿Cómo lo saben?*

   Teacher Tip
   Use a strategy such as *Think, Pair, Share* to give children time to think on their own before discussing their thinking with others.

2. Have the class choose an object in the room to measure. Choose a child to help you measure the object. Discuss:

   (?) **If** [Rosalie] **and I each measure the** [bulletin board] **with our hands, do you think our measurements will be the same? Why or why not?**

(¿) *Si* [Rosalie] *y yo medimos cada uno* [el tablero de anuncios] *con nuestras manos, ¿creen que nuestras medidas serán iguales? ¿Por qué?*

3. Each of you measure the object as the class counts the number of hands. Record the measurements. Discuss:

(?) **Are our measurements the same? Why did it take more of** [Rosalie's] **hands to measure the** [bulletin board]?

(¿) *¿Son sus medidas iguales? ¿Por qué necesitamos más manos de* [Rosalie] *para medir* [el tablero de anuncios]?

Extend the Experience

As a class, decide how to share and display the **At Home** activities. Some ideas include:

- Bind the **At Home** activities together to make a class book. Consider captioning each **At Home** activity, using a sentence frame such as, "[Julia, Julia] what do you see? I see a [chair] that [daddy] measured with me."

- Pair children with older buddies from another class. Have the younger children share their **At Home** activities with their older buddies. Have the older buddies take the role of home partner and do the **At Home** activity with their younger partners.

Handy Measurements

Dear Family,

Our class is learning about measurement. We measured objects in the classroom with our hands. This helped us learn to:

- measure length using units (hands)
- use math words such as *longer* and *height*.

In this activity, the two of you will measure the length of two objects in your home using your hands. In class, we will discuss your measurements.

1 Collect the things you need.
- A pencil, pen, or crayon

2 Talk about measuring with hands at school.

3 Do the activity.

- Walk around your home and find an object to measure.

- Each of you measure the object with your hands.

Talk about:
- Did it take more of your hands or more of my hands to measure the object? Why do you think that happened?

4 Draw a picture of the object and write its length in child's hands and in home partner's hands.

First Object:

Child's hands _____   Home Partner's hands _____

5 Do the activity again with a different object.

Second Object:

Child's hands _____   Home Partner's hands _____

6 Write your thoughts about this activity.

Dear Teacher:

_____

_____

_____

From, _____
(child's name)

_____
(home partner's name)

7 Get ready for school.
Talk about:

• Which of our objects is longer? Why do you think so?

Medidas muy a la mano

Estimada familia:

Nuestra clase está aprendiendo acerca de las medidas. Medimos objetos en la clase con nuestras manos. Esto nos ayudó a aprender a:

* medir longitud usando unidades (las manos)
* usar palabras matemáticas como *más largo y altura*.

En esta actividad, ustedes dos van a medir en su casa la longitud de dos objetos usando sus manos. En clase, comentaremos sus medidas.

① Reúnan las cosas que necesiten.

* Un lápiz, una pluma o un creyón

② Hablen sobre medir con las manos en la escuela.

¿Qué mediste en la escuela con tus manos?

Medimos la mesa de ciencias. Mide quince manos mías de larga.

③ Hagan la actividad.

* Caminen por la casa y busquen un objeto para medir.

12:00

* Cada uno mide el objeto con sus manos.

Hablen sobre:

* ¿Necesitamos más manos tuyas o más manos mías para medir el objeto? ¿Por qué crees que pasó eso?

4 Hagan un dibujo del objeto y escriban su longitud en manos de niño y en manos del compañero en casa.

Primer objeto:

Manos de niño _____

Manos del compañero en casa _____

5 Háganlo otra vez con un objeto distinto.

Segundo objeto:

Manos de niño _____

Manos del compañero en casa _____

6 Escriban lo que piensan sobre esta actividad.

Estimado maestro:

_____

_____

_____

De, _____
(nombre del niño)

_____
(nombre del compañero en casa)

7 Prepárense para la escuela. Hablen sobre:

• ¿Cuál de nuestros objetos es el más largo? ¿Por qué crees eso?

Geometry Activities Overview

GEOMETRY CONCEPTS

Children seem to develop early geometric ideas in stages. They first learn to recognize whole shapes and then begin to recognize their attributes. Later, they see relationships between shapes. The **MathLinks** activities help children develop these concepts and provide experiences combining and subdividing shapes.

Recognize and Describe Shapes

Young children first recognize shapes by their appearance as a whole. They identify a triangle, for example, because "it looks like an ice cream cone." Because children initially recognize shapes by their appearance, if they are exposed to one type of triangle only, often the equilateral triangle, they develop the misunderstanding that just this shape is a triangle.

Young children need many opportunities to explore shapes to internalize their properties. They need experience with multiple examples of a shape, and benefit from opportunities to discuss nonexamples and compare them with examples of the shape. In the first two **MathLinks** geometry activities, "Triangle Fun" and "Triangle Puzzles," children explore both examples and nonexamples of triangles. Many types, sizes, and orientations are presented so that children's understanding of triangles encompasses more than the equilateral triangle. In "Fold a Square," children fold a square to create and discuss the attributes of new shapes

(i.e., squares, rectangles, triangles, and trapezoids).

As children explore shapes and their characteristics, they begin to construct definitions for them. In the **MathLinks** geometry activities, children informally explore the following shapes:

- **TRIANGLE:** A shape with three straight sides.

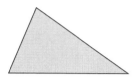

- **QUADRILATERAL:** A shape with four straight sides. The following shapes are types of quadrilaterals and are defined by adding conditions:

- **Trapezoid:** A shape with exactly one pair of parallel sides.

- **Parallelogram:** A shape with two pairs of parallel sides.

- **Rectangle:** A shape with two pairs of parallel sides and four right angles. A rectangle is a special type of parallelogram. All rectangles are parallelograms, but not all parallelograms are rectangles.

MathLinks

- **Rhombus:** A shape with four equal sides. A rhombus is a special type of parallelogram. A rhombus with 90° angles is also a square. All rhombi are parallelograms but not all parallelograms are rhombi.

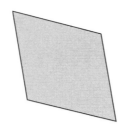

- **Square:** A shape with four equal sides and four right angles. A square is a special type of rhombus, rectangle, and parallelogram but not all variations of these shapes are squares.

geometric properties and develop spatial reasoning, spatial visualization, and spatial memory. In the activity "Triangle Fun," children explore ways to combine two triangles to make new shapes. In "Triangle Puzzles," children cut a triangle into two pieces to make a rectangle puzzle. In "Fold a Square," children divide a square into several shapes by folding it twice.

Combine and Subdivide Shapes

Important to children's exploration of shapes are experiences decomposing them and creating new shapes. Such explorations help children learn about

Learning about Geometry

The following table identifies the specific geometry concepts developed in each of the activities. A solid bullet (●) identifies the main focus of an activity and an open bullet (○) identifies other concepts developed.

	1. Triangle Fun	2. Triangle Puzzles	3. Fold a Square
Recognize and describe shapes and their attributes	●	●	●
Explore different sizes and variations of triangles	●	○	○
Combine and subdivide shapes	●	●	●
Explore spatial relationships	○	●	●
Use mathematical language	●	●	●

WORKING TOGETHER

In the **MathLinks** activities, children work with partners at school and at home. The goal is to enhance their mathematical development while at the same time helping them learn to work together successfully, communicate effectively, and be responsible learners.

Work with Others

Most kindergarten children are ready to begin to work with a partner. The focus of the **MathLinks** geometry activities is for children to share the work, help each other, and make decisions together.

Communicate Thinking

All of the **MathLinks** activities provide frequent opportunities for children to discuss their thinking with school and home partners and with the class. Children learn to communicate about mathematics and about how they work together. They also learn to explain their thinking and listen to the thinking of others. In the **MathLinks** geometry activities, children work and talk with partners and exchange their ideas during whole-class discussions. Children also record and discuss their results, which helps them learn to organize and communicate mathematical ideas.

Be Responsible

Helping children learn to be responsible means giving them opportunities to assume responsibility and helping them acquire strategies to do so successfully. Children's understanding of what it means to be responsible and how to be responsible develops over time, with many experiences, and with opportunities to talk about them. **MathLinks** helps children be responsible for:

- their learning and behavior in school and at home
- getting the home activities to and from home
- finding a home partner and completing the activities
- at times, teaching something to a home partner
- explaining to others what they did at school and at home.

Learning to Work Together

The following table identifies the social skills focus of each activity. A solid bullet (●) identifies the main focus, and an open bullet (○) identifies other skills children might practice.

	1. Triangle Fun	2. Triangle Puzzles	3. Fold a Square
Share the work	●	●	●
Make decisions together	●	○	○
Help each other	○	●	●

GEOMETRY ACTIVITIES AT A GLANCE

The following is a summary of each of the geometry activities.

1. Triangle Fun

Children discuss and define triangles. Each child picks a triangle from an envelope and finds a partner with a matching triangle. Partners put their triangles together to make a new shape and then classify their new shape as a triangle or not a triangle. Children and their home partners find objects that are shaped like triangles and objects that are not shaped like triangles and record their results. Back at school, pairs discuss the **At Home** activity and then combine their results from home to make a book.

2. Triangle Puzzles

Children cut triangles into two pieces to make puzzles. Partners then exchange and assemble each other's puzzle. Children and their home partners each make a triangle puzzle. They exchange and assemble each other's puzzle. They then combine their four puzzle pieces to make a rectangle. Back at school, partners combine the triangle puzzles they made at home to make a rectangle puzzle.

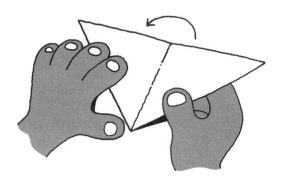

3. Fold a Square

Pairs fold a square two times. They unfold the square, identify the shapes made by the folds, and color in the shapes. Children and their home partners do the same, discuss the shapes they make, and send the square back to school. Back at school, children make puzzles by cutting out the shapes on their paper squares from home. Partners assemble each other's puzzle.

LITERATURE LINKS

***The Shape of Things* by Dayle Ann Dodds** (Candlewick Press, 1996). With its colorful illustrations and rhymes, this story helps children identify shapes found on objects in their environment. Consider using this book to introduce the activity "Triangle Fun" to help children become familiar with triangles and other shapes.

***Shape Space* by Cathryn Falwell** (Clarion Books, 1992). In this book, a young girl comes upon a box filled with shapes. As she dances among the colorful shapes, she discovers each shape's attributes. She learns to combine the shapes in imaginative ways creating a hat, a skirt, a dancing partner–even a whole town. Consider using this book to help children become familiar with triangles and other shapes and to introduce the activity, "Triangle Puzzles."

***Bear in a Square* by Stella Blackstone** (Barefoot Books, 1998). Through rhymes, children follow a friendly bear searching for shapes in colorful settings such as a pool, a cave, and a park. Using this book to introduce "Fold a Square" will help children find shapes inside other shapes.

¿Dónde está el triángulo? by Pascale de Bourgoing and Colette Camil (La Galera, 1997).

Readers follow a carpenter bird on a walk as he looks for objects that are shaped like triangles, such as a sail on a boat, a sign, and a mountain. At the end of the book, readers are encouraged to discover other objects in their environment that are shaped like triangles.

Consider reading this book to children before beginning the **MathLinks** geometry activities.

Spot's Big Book of Colors, Shapes, and Number/El libro grande de Spot colores, formas y números by Eric Hill

(Ventura Publishing Ltd., 1994). With the help of a dog named Spot, this book introduces children to colors, shapes, and numbers in Spanish and English. This book can be used to introduce shapes before beginning the **MathLinks** geometry activities.

Triangle Fun

AT SCHOOL

Children discuss and define triangles. Each child picks a triangle from an envelope and then finds a partner with a matching triangle. Partners put their triangles together to make a shape and then classify their new shape as a triangle or not a triangle.

AT HOME

Children and their home partners find objects that are shaped like triangles and objects that are not shaped like triangles and record their results.

BACK AT SCHOOL

Partners discuss the **At Home** activity, then combine their results from home to make a book.

Learning About Geometry

In this activity, children:

- recognize and describe shapes and their attributes
- explore different sizes and variations of triangles
- combine shapes to make other shapes.

Learning to Work Together

In this activity, children:

- share the work
- make decisions together

Mathematical Vocabulary

shape	figura
rhombus	rombo
triangle	triángulo
side	lado
vertex	vértice

Teacher Tip

**Triangles
in the Envelope:**
You need matching
triangles for every
two children. If you
have twenty chil-
dren, make two
copies of each "Tri-
angles 1," "Triangles
2," pp. 169–170. Cut
out the triangles,
mix them up, and
put them in the
envelope.

For a different class
size, be sure to have
two matching
triangles for every
two children. If you
have an odd number
of children, you will
need one set of three
matching triangles to
form a group of
three.

**Triangles
for Modeling:**
You will need
four triangles for
modeling. Make two
copies of "Triangles
1," p. 169. For **Make
Connections**, cut
out and use two
triangles that are
different. For
**Explain and Model
the Activity**, cut
out and use two
triangles that are
the same.

AT SCHOOL

Get Ready

Prepare materials:

- A copy of the Geometry Activities
  Family Letter, p. 17, for each child.
  You may want to attach it to the
  At Home activity.

- A copy of the **At Home** activity,
  with the return date written on it,
  for each child

- Triangles for each pair in an envelope (See **Teacher Tip**.)

- Four paper triangles for modeling
  (See **Teacher Tip.**)

- A sheet of paper for each pair,
  plus one for modeling

- A pencil and glue for each pair

Literature Link
The Shape of Things
by Dayle Ann Dodds
(Candlewick Press,
1996). Introduce the
activity with this
book to help children
become familiar with
triangles and other
shapes. Note: You
may want to use the
correct mathematical
term *rhombus* in
place of *diamond*
while reading this
book. (optional)

Make Connections

1. Show the class the two different triangles.
   Discuss:

Whole Class

(?) **What do you notice about these two
shapes?** (Be sure to call the triangles *shapes*
when asking this question so that children have
the opportunity to point out that both shapes are
triangles.)

(?) **What is the same about these two shapes?
What is different?**

(¿) *¿Qué notan de estas dos figuras?* (Asegúrese de
llamar a los triángulos figuras cuando haga esta
pregunta para que los niños tengan la oportunidad
de decir que las dos figuras son triángulos).

(¿) *¿En qué se parecen estas dos figuras? ¿En qué se
diferencian?*

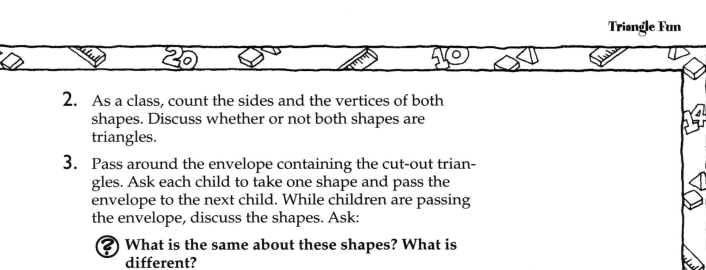

2. As a class, count the sides and the vertices of both shapes. Discuss whether or not both shapes are triangles.

3. Pass around the envelope containing the cut-out triangles. Ask each child to take one shape and pass the envelope to the next child. While children are passing the envelope, discuss the shapes. Ask:

(?) **What is the same about these shapes? What is different?**

(?) **What shapes are these? How do you know?**

(¿) *¿En qué se parecen estas figuras? ¿En qué se diferencian?*

(¿) *¿Qué figuras son éstas? ¿Cómo lo saben?*

4. Explain that children will find a partner by walking around the room and finding someone with a matching triangle. Discuss:

(?) **How can you find out if your triangle is the same as someone else's? Show us. What is another way?**

(?) **How can we be responsible as we walk around the room?**

(?) **What's a friendly way to greet your partner?**

(¿) *¿Cómo pueden averiguar si su triángulo es igual al de alguien más? Muéstrennos. ¿Hay otra manera de averiguarlo? Si es así, ¿cuál es?*

(¿) *¿Cómo podemos ser responsables mientras caminamos por la clase?*

(¿) *¿Cómo pueden saludar amablemente a su compañero?*

5. Have children find their partners.

Explain and Model the Activity

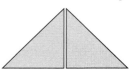

Activity Directions

Pairs:

- find ways to combine their triangles to make shapes. Triangles must have one of their sides touching.

- decide on one of the ways to combine their triangles

- glue their triangles in this shape to a sheet of paper and write their names on it.

Teacher Tip

Children may call a rhombus a *diamond*. Explain that the mathematical name for the shape is *rhombus*.

Choose a pair to demonstrate the activity as you give the directions. As the pair models, ask:

Whole Class in Pairs

(?) **What shape did you make with your triangles? Is it a triangle? How do you know?**

(?) **How else can you combine your triangles?**

(?) **How are you sharing the work?**

(¿) *¿Qué figura formaron con sus triángulos? ¿Es un triángulo? ¿Cómo lo saben?*

(¿) *¿De qué otra manera pueden combinar sus triángulos?*

(¿) *¿Cómo están compartiendo el trabajo?*

Pair Work

1. Distribute materials to each pair.

2. Have pairs do the activity. Circulate and talk with them about their work and their thinking:

Children Working in Pairs

(?) **What shapes have you made from the two triangles?**

(?) **How will you choose the shape to glue to the paper?**

(?) **How are you sharing the work?**

(¿) *¿Qué figuras han formado con los dos triángulos?*

(¿) *¿Cómo van a escoger la figura que van a pegar en el papel?*

(¿) *¿Cómo están compartiendo el trabajo?*

Report and Reflect

Whole Class in Pairs

1. Explain that pairs that made triangles will sit on one side of the room and pairs that made shapes that are not triangles will sit on the other. Have pairs decide where they belong

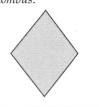

and move to that side of the room. Ask pairs to place their new shapes in front of them so all can see.

2. Have some pairs describe their shape to the class. Ask one or more of the following questions:

(?) What would you like to tell the class about your shape?

(?) Is your shape a triangle? How do you know?

(?) If your shape is not a triangle, does your shape have a name? How do you know your shape is a [rectangle]?

(?) How did you and your partner choose the shape to glue to the paper? Did you have any problems making this decision? What did you do to solve them? How did that work?

(¿) *¿Qué les gustaría decir a la clase acerca de sus figuras?*

(¿) *¿Es su figura un triángulo? ¿Cómo lo saben?*

(¿) *Si su figura no es un triángulo, ¿tiene su figura un nombre? ¿Cómo saben que su figura es un [rectángulo]?*

(¿) *¿Cómo escogieron tú y tu compañero la figura para pegar en el papel? ¿Tuvieron algún problema tomando esta decisión? ¿Qué hicieron para resolverlo? ¿Cómo les fue?*

3. First in pairs, then as a class, discuss:

(?) How are the triangles and the other shapes the same? How are they different?

(?) Do we have more triangles or other shapes? How do you know?

(¿) *¿En qué se parecen los triángulos y las otras figuras? ¿En qué se diferencian?*

(¿) *¿Tenemos más triángulos u otras figuras? ¿Cómo lo saben?*

Teacher Tip
Use a strategy such as *Think, Pair, Share* to give children time to think on their own before discussing their thinking with others.

Prepare for Success at Home

1. Show and explain the **At Home** activity. Explain that children and their home partners will find, draw, and write about objects shaped like triangles and objects not shaped like triangles. Ask:

    ? **When is a good time to ask your home partner to help you? Why is that a good time?**

    ? **What is something in your house that is shaped like a triangle? What is something that is not shaped like a triangle?**

    ¿ *¿Cuándo es un buen momento para pedir ayuda a su compañero en casa? ¿Por qué es ése un buen momento?*

    ¿ *¿Hay algo en su casa que tenga forma de triángulo? ¿Hay algo que no tenga forma de triángulo?*

2. Explain when children are to bring their **At Home** activities back to class and that, in pairs, they will use them to make books. Discuss:

    ? **How many days do you have to do this activity?**

    ? **What will help you remember to bring your At Home Activity back so that you and you partner will be able to make your book?**

    ¿ *¿Cuántos días tienen para hacer esta actividad?*

    ¿ *¿Qué les ayudará a recordar a llevar de vuelta a clase su Actividad en casa para que tú y tu compañero puedan hacer su libro?*

Whole Class

BACK AT SCHOOL

Get Ready

1. Collect and review the **At Home** activities.

2. Determine how you will select partners.

3. Prepare materials:

   • Scissors for each pair

   • Several staplers for the class

Discuss the At Home Activity

**Whole Class
in Pairs**

1. Select pairs and have partners sit together.
   Return the **At Home** activities to children.
   First in pairs, then as a class, discuss:

   **(?) Who was your home partner? When did
   you ask that person to be your home partner?
   How did that work?**

   **(?) How did you decide on the shapes for your book
   pages?**

   *(¿) ¿Quién fue su compañero en casa? ¿Cuándo pidieron a
   esa persona que fuera su compañero? ¿Cómo les fue?*

   *(¿) ¿Cómo decidieron las figuras para las páginas de
   su libro?*

2. Ask pairs to read their pages to each other, cut them
   out, and decide on an order for them. Have them staple
   the pages together to make a book. Discuss:

   **(?) What are ways to help your partner if he or she
   does not know a word?**

   **(?) How can you decide on an order for your pages?
   What's another way?**

   *(¿) ¿De qué manera pueden ayudar a su compañero si él o
   ella no sabe una palabra?*

   *(¿) ¿Cómo pueden decidir un orden para sus páginas? ¿Hay
   alguna otra manera de hacerlo? Si es así, ¿cuál es?*

3. As a class, discuss:

(?) **Name an object in your book that is not shaped like a triangle? What shape is it?**

(?) **How are the [square] and the triangle in your book the same? How are they different?**

(¿) *Nombren un objeto en su libro que no tenga la forma de un triángulo. ¿Qué figura es?*

(¿) *¿En qué se parecen el [cuadrado] y el triángulo de su libro? ¿En qué se diferencian?*

4. As a class, decide what to do with the books. Some ideas include putting them in the classroom library, reading the books to older buddies, putting them all together to make a class book, or displaying them in the classroom.

Extend the Experience

- Have each child make an "I found a _____ on a _____" book for other shapes.

- Take a walk and find objects shaped like triangles in nature, the school yard, or the neighborhood.

- Construct different types of triangles using straws, pencils, markers, pipe cleaners, or crayons.

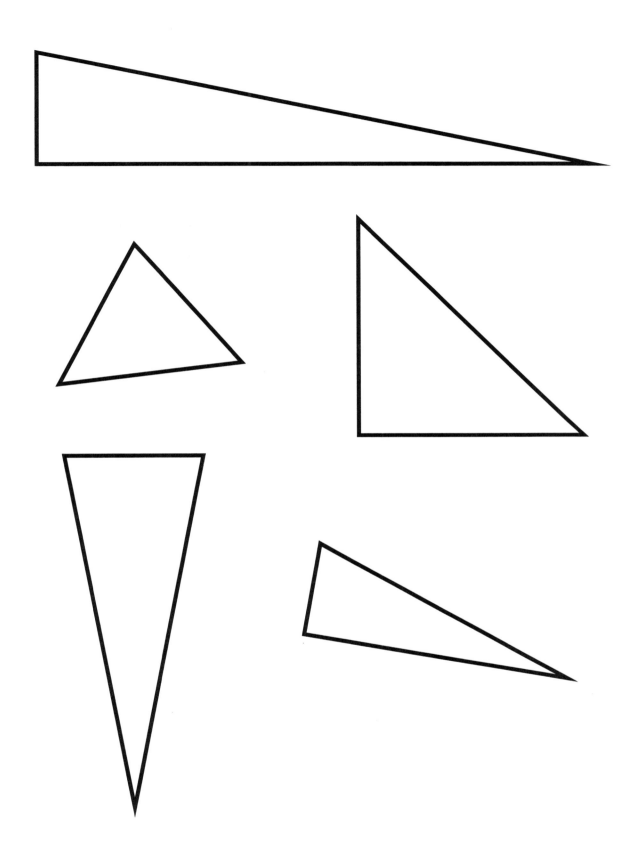

Triangles 2

Triangle Fun

Dear Family,

Our class is learning about geometry. We discussed triangles and made shapes with triangles. This helped us learn to:

- put shapes together to make other shapes
- use math words such as *side* and *vertices* (corners).

In this **At Home** activity, the two of you will find things shaped like triangles and things not shaped like triangles. You will make book pages with this information. In class, partners will combine their pages to make books.

① Collect the things you need.

- A pencil, pen, or crayon

② Talk about the triangle activity at school.

③ Do the activity.

- Walk around your home and look for triangles or things that are shaped like triangles.

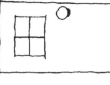

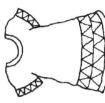

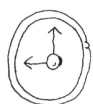

- Look for shapes that are not triangles or objects that are not shaped like triangles.

Talk about:

- How do we know this shape is a triangle? How many sides does a triangle have? How many vertices?
- How many sides does that shape have? How many vertices? What else is shaped like that?

4 Draw one of the objects you found and complete the sentence on each "book" page below. (**Please print.**)

Book Pages

We found a "triangle"

on a _____

We found a

on a _____

We found a

on a _____

5 Write your thoughts about this activity.

Dear Teacher:

_____

_____

_____

From,

_____
(child's name)

_____
(home partner's name)

6 Get ready for school. Practice reading your book pages. Read to your grandfather, your aunt, or even the dog! **Talk about:**

• Are you ready to read your book pages to a partner at school?

Diversión con *triángulos*

Estimada familia:

Nuestra clase está aprendiendo acerca de la geometría.
Hablamos de los triángulos y formamos figuras con triángulos.
Esto nos ayudó a aprender a:

• juntar figuras para hacer otras figuras

• usar palabras matemáticas como *lado* y *vértices* (esquinas).

En esta Actividad en casa, ustedes dos buscarán cosas con forma de triángulo y cosas sin forma de triángulo. Ustedes van a hacer las páginas de un libro con esta información. En clase, los compañeros combinarán sus páginas para hacer los libros.

1 Reúnan las cosas que necesiten.

• Un lápiz, una pluma o un creyón

2 Hablen sobre la actividad de triángulos de la escuela.

3 Hagan la actividad.

• Caminen por su casa y busquen triángulos o cosas con forma de triángulo.

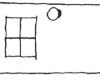

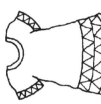

• Busquen figuras que no sean triángulos u objetos que no tengan forma de triángulo.

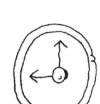

Hablen sobre:

• ¿Cómo sabemos que esta figura es un triángulo? ¿Cuántos lados tiene un triángulo? ¿Cuántas vértices?

• ¿Cuántos lados tiene esa figura? ¿Cuántas vértices? ¿Qué más tiene esa forma?

4 Dibujen uno de los objetos que encontraron y completen la oración de cada página de "libro" a continuación. (Por favor escriban con letra de molde.)

Páginas de libro

Encontramos un "triángulo" _____ en _____

Encontramos un _____ en _____.

Encontramos un _____ en _____.

5 Escriban lo que piensan sobre esta actividad.

Estimado maestro:

_____
_____
_____

De, _____
(nombre del niño)

_____
(nombre del compañero en casa)

6 Prepárense para la escuela. Practica leyendo tus páginas de libro. Lee a tu abuelo, a tu tía o ¡hasta al perro! Hablen sobre:

- ¿Estás preparado para leer tus páginas de libro a un compañero de la escuela?

Triangle Puzzles

AT SCHOOL

Children cut triangles into two pieces to make puzzles. Partners then exchange and assemble each other's puzzles.

AT HOME

Children and their home partners each cut a triangle to make a puzzle. They exchange and assemble each other's puzzle. They then combine their four puzzle pieces to make a rectangle. Finally, they choose one of the triangle puzzles to send back to school.

BACK AT SCHOOL

Partners combine the triangle puzzles they made at home to make a rectangle puzzle.

Learning About Geometry

In this activity, children:

- recognize and describe shapes and their attributes
- combine and subdivide shapes
- explore spatial relationships.

Learning to Work Together

In this activity, children:

- share the work
- help each other.

Mathematical Vocabulary

rectangle   rectángulo

AT SCHOOL

Get Ready

1. Determine how you will select partners. (See **Forming Pairs,** p. 20.)

2. Prepare materials:

   - A copy of the **At Home** activity, with the return date written on it, for each child.

   - An envelope attached to each **At Home** activity

   - A copy of "Home Triangle Puzzles," p. 188, for each child, attached to the **At Home** activity. (Children will cut out the puzzles at school and put them in the envelopes to take home.)

   - A copy of "Home Puzzle Frames," p. 189, for each child, attached to the **At Home** activity

   - A copy of each page of "Is It a Triangle?," pp. 183–185, for the teacher (for **Make Connections**)

   - A copy of each "School Triangle Puzzles," pp. 186–187, for each pair and a copy to use for modeling

   - Scissors for each child

   - Glue for each pair

Literature Link

Shape Space by Cathryn Falwell (Clarion Books, 1992). Introduce the activity with this book to help children become familiar with triangles and other shapes. (optional)

Make Connections

1. Select pairs and have partners sit together. Introduce this activity by displaying one of the "Is It a Triangle?" pages. Have pairs discuss the shapes and determine which is a triangle and which is not. Do the same for the other two "Is It a Triangle?" pages. First in pairs, then as a class, discuss:

   Whole Class in Pairs

   (?) **Are these shapes both triangles? How do you know?**

   (?) **Why is this shape a triangle and this shape not a triangle?**

(?) How could you make this shape into a triangle?

(¿) *¿Son estas dos figuras triángulos? ¿Cómo lo saben?*

(¿) *¿Por qué es esta figura un triángulo y ésta no es un triángulo?*

(¿) *¿Cómo podrían hacer un triángulo con esta figura?*

Explain and Model the Activity

1. Show the "School Triangle Puzzles" and explain that each partner will make a triangle puzzle by cutting out a triangle, cutting the triangle into two puzzle pieces, exchanging the puzzle pieces with a partner, and then putting the partner's puzzle together.

2. Choose a child to be your partner. Model the activity as you explain the directions one at a time. As you model, ask your partner:

   (?) How can we turn the pieces so that they will make a triangle again? What is another way?

   (¿) *¿Cómo podemos girar las piezas para que formen otra vez un triángulo? ¿Hay otra manera de hacerlo? Si es así, ¿cuál es?*

3. Ask the class:

   (?) If you are having trouble putting the pieces together, what can you do?

   (?) If your partner asks for help, how can you help without doing the puzzle for him?

   (¿) *Si tienen problemas armando las piezas, ¿qué pueden hacer?*

   (¿) *Si su compañero pide ayuda, ¿cómo pueden ayudarle sin hacer su rompecabezas?*

Activity Directions

Each partner:

- writes his name on the "School Triangle Puzzles 1" (Each partner in a pair should have a different triangle puzzle sheet.)
- cuts along the dotted line that separates the two triangles on the page
- cuts out the shaded triangle
- makes one fold anywhere on the shaded triangle
- unfolds the triangle and cuts on the crease to make two puzzle pieces.

Partners then :

- exchange puzzles
- assemble their partner's puzzle using their partner's puzzle frame as a guide
- discuss the puzzles to decide if the pieces are in the right place. When both partners agree that the puzzles are assembled correctly, they glue the pieces in the frames.

Pair Work

1. Distribute materials to each pair.

2. Have pairs do the activity. Circulate and talk with them about their work and their thinking:

Children Working in Pairs

(?) **Are any of your puzzle pieces triangles? How do you know? What shapes are your other puzzle pieces? Do you have any shapes that you can't name?**

(?) (Point to a shape.) **How many [vertices] does this puzzle piece have?**

(?) **How are you sharing the work? Is that fair to both of you?**

(¿) *¿Son algunas piezas de su rompecabezas triángulos? ¿Cómo lo saben? ¿Qué otras formas tienen sus otras piezas de rompecabezas? ¿Tienen algunas figuras que no puedan nombrar?*

(¿) Señale una figura. *¿Cuántas [vértices] tiene esta pieza de rompecabezas?*

(¿) *¿Cómo están compartiendo el trabajo? ¿Es eso justo para los dos?*

Report and Reflect

1. First in pairs, then as a class, discuss:

Whole Class in Pairs

(?) **How did you figure out how to put your pieces back together?**

(?) **What is a way that you helped your partner or your partner helped you?**

(¿) *¿Cómo averiguaron cómo armar sus piezas de nuevo?*

(¿) *¿En qué manera ayudaron a su compañero o cómo les ayudó su compañero?*

Prepare for Success at Home

Whole Class

1. Show and explain the **At Home** activity. Explain that children and their home partners will make triangle puzzles and put them together.

   (?) **Who will you ask to be your home partner?**

   (?) **What will you and your home partner do?**

   (¿) *¿A quién van a pedir que sea su compañero en casa?*

   (¿) *¿Qué van a hacer tu compañero en casa y tú?*

2. Give each pair an "Home Triangle Puzzles" p. 188. Have pairs cut out the triangles along the dotted lines and each put two of the triangles in the envelope attached to their **At Home** activity.

3. Explain when children are to bring their **At Home** activities and puzzles back to class and that the puzzles will be used in class to make rectangle puzzles. Discuss:

   (?) **Why is it important to bring your puzzle back to class?**

   (?) **What will help you to get the puzzle pieces back to school?**

   (¿) *¿Por qué es importante traer de vuelta a clase su rompecabezas?*

   (¿) *¿Qué les va a ayudar a recordar que tienen que traer a la escuela las piezas del rompecabezas?*

BACK AT SCHOOL

Get Ready

1. Collect and review the **At Home** activities.

2. Check to make sure children's envelopes with puzzle pieces are labeled with their names.

3. Determine how you will select partners.

4. Prepare materials:

- A copy of "Rectangle Puzzle Frame," p. 190, for each pair
- Glue for each pair

Discuss the At Home Activity

1. Select pairs and have partners sit together. Return the **At Home** activities and envelopes with puzzle pieces to children. Discuss:

Whole Class in Pairs

(?) What shapes are your puzzle pieces? How do you know?

(?) What happened when you and your partner tried to put your triangle puzzles together?

(?) What did you do that helped you get your puzzle pieces back to school?

(¿) ¿Qué figuras son sus piezas de rompecabezas? ¿Cómo lo saben?

(¿) ¿Qué pasó cuando tú y tu compañero intentaron armar sus piezas de rompecabezas?

(¿) ¿Qué hicieron para recordar traer a la escuela sus piezas de rompecabezas?

2. Show a "Rectangle Puzzle Frame," and explain that pairs will use it to make a rectangle puzzle with all four of their puzzle pieces from home.

Children Working in Pairs

3. Distribute materials to each pair. Have pairs make the puzzles and glue the pieces to the frame.

4. Have pairs show their puzzles to the class. Discuss:

Whole Class in Pairs

(?) How did you and your partner share the work?

(?) Did you have any problems putting the pieces together to make a rectangle? If so, what happened? How did you figure it out?

Teacher Tip
Use a strategy such as *Turn to Your Partner* to give all the children a chance to think and talk about the questions.

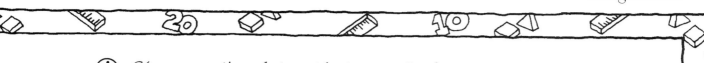

(¿) *¿Cómo compartieron la tarea tú y tu compañero?*

(¿) *¿Tuvieron algún problema armando las piezas para formar un rectángulo? Si fue así, ¿qué pasó? ¿Cómo lo averiguaron?*

Extend the Experience

- Have pairs make puzzles with shapes other than a triangle.

- Have partners each put pattern blocks together to make a shape, then copy each other's shape.

- Provide opportunities for children to freely explore Tangram puzzle pieces. Tangram sets are available commercially through companies that sell mathematics manipulatives.

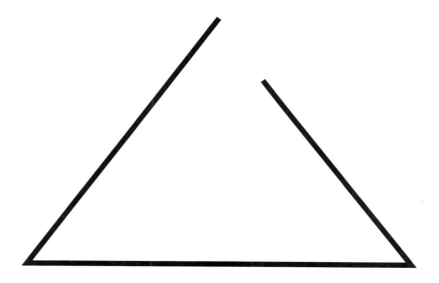

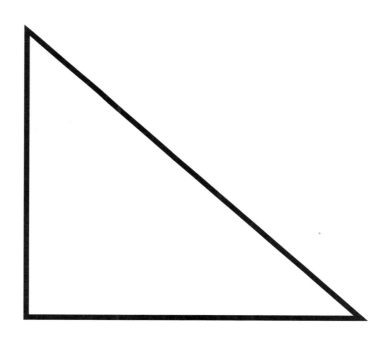

Is It a Triangle? 1 183

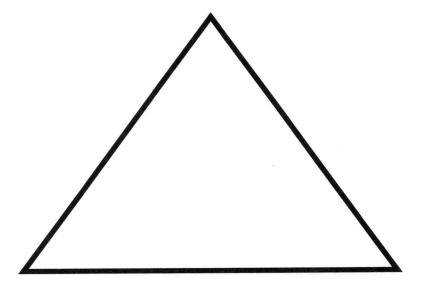

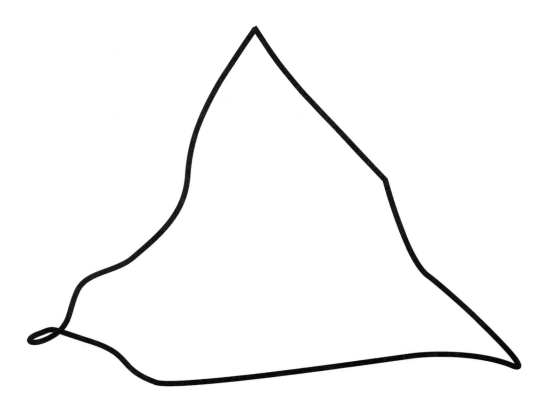

Is It a Triangle? 2

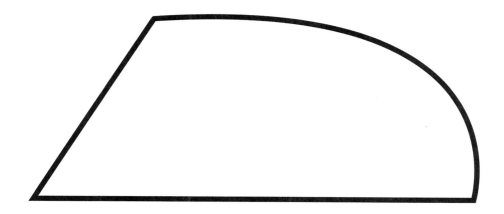

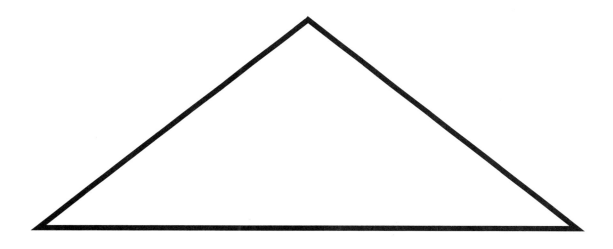

Is It a Triangle? 3

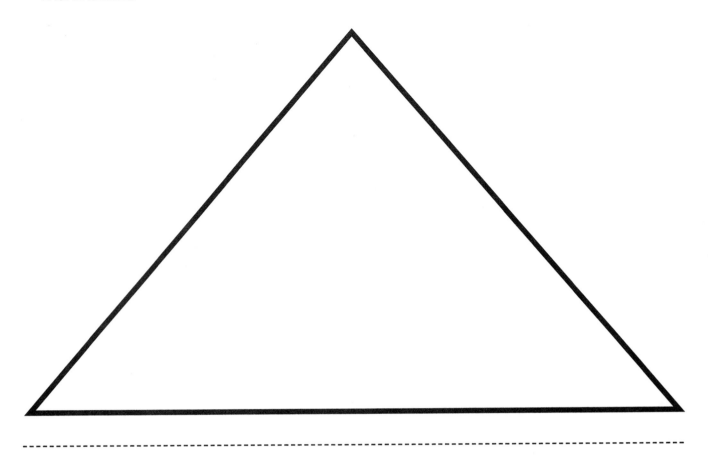

School Triangle Puzzles 1

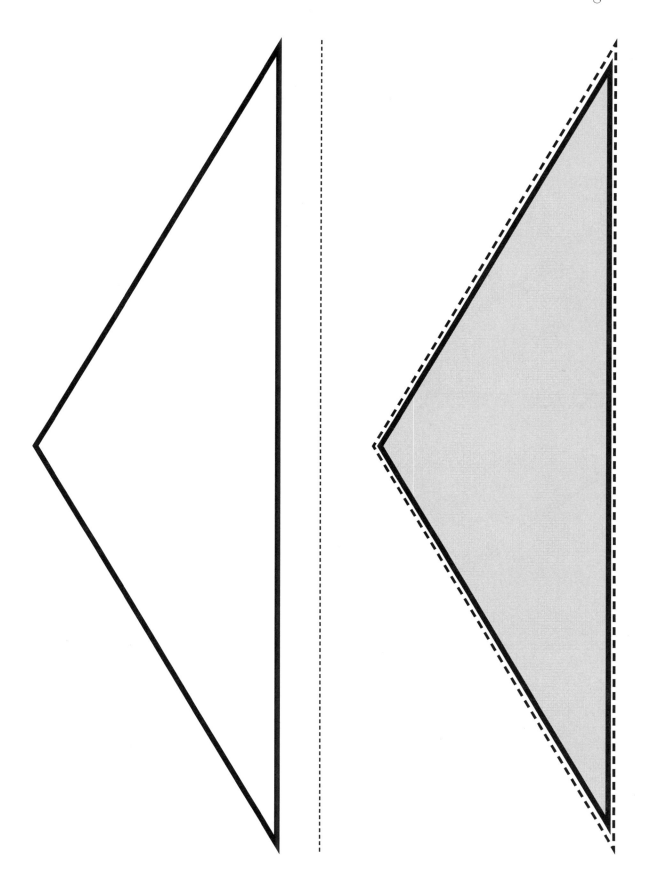

School Triangle Puzzles 2

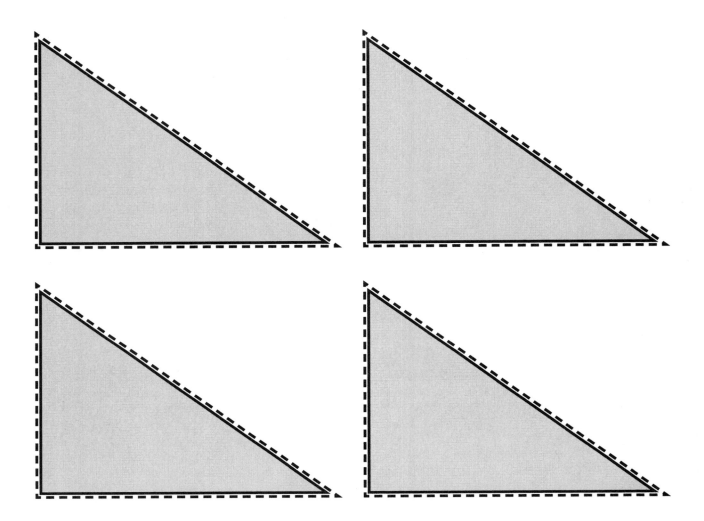

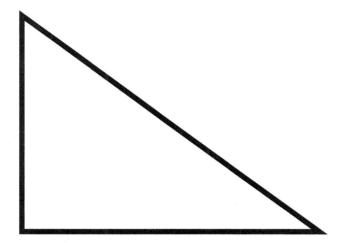

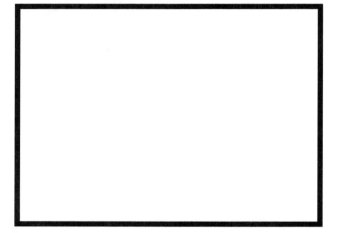

Rectangle Puzzle Frame

Triangle Puzzles

Child's Name:

Return Date:

Dear Family,

Our class is learning about geometry. We made and put triangle puzzles together. This helped us learn to:

- understand that shapes can be made from other shapes
- use math words such as *side* and *vertex* (corner).

In this activity, each of you will make a triangle puzzle. You will put each other's puzzle together. Then, you will use both of your puzzles to make a bigger rectangle puzzle. You will choose one of the triangle puzzles to send back to school.

❶ Collect the things you need.

- A pencil, pen, or crayon
- The two triangles from the attached envelope
- Home Puzzle Frames
- Scissors (optional)

❷ Talk about putting puzzles together.

❸ Make the puzzles.

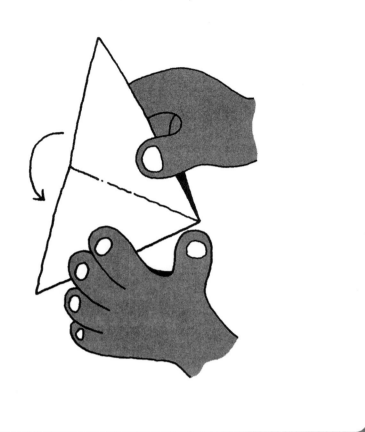

Each of you:

- Take one of the triangles from the envelope
- Make one fold anywhere on the triangle
- Unfold the triangle and cut or carefully tear it on the fold
- Write your name on the back of each piece.

MathLinks At Home Activity

4 Trade puzzles. One at a time, put each other's puzzle together. Use the triangle frame on the "At Home Activity Puzzle Frames" as a guide.

5 Put both triangle puzzles together to make a rectangle. Use the rectangle frame on the "At Home Activity Puzzle Frames" as a guide.

6 Write your thoughts about this activity.

Dear Teacher:

_____

_____

_____

_____

From,

_____

(child's name)

_____

(home partner's name)

7 Get ready for school. Choose one of the triangle puzzles and put it in the envelope to return to school. Talk about:

• Which puzzle do you want to take back to school?

Rompecabezas de triángulos

Estimada familia:

Nuestra clase está aprendiendo acerca de la geometría. Hicimos y armamos rompecabezas de triángulos. Esto nos ayudó a:

- entender que con figuras se pueden hacer otras figuras
- usar palabras matemáticas como *lado y vértice* (esquina).

En esta Actividad en casa, cada uno va a hacer un rompecabezas de un triángulo. Ustedes armarán sus rompecabezas entre sí. Entonces, usarán sus dos rompecabezas para hacer un rompecabezas más grande de rectángulo. Escogerán uno de los rompecabezas de triángulos para mandar a la escuela.

1 Reúnan las cosas que necesiten.

- Un lápiz, una pluma o un creyón
- Los dos triángulos incluidos en el sobre
- Marcos de rompecabezas (Home Puzzle Frames)
- Tijeras (*opcional*)

2 Hablen sobre armar los rompecabezas.

3 Armen los rompecabezas.

Cada uno:

- Saquen uno de los triángulos del sobre.
- Hagan un pliegue en cualquier parte del triángulo.
- Desdoblen el triángulo y recorten o rasguen con cuidado por la marca del pliegue.
- Escriban su nombre por detrás de cada pieza.

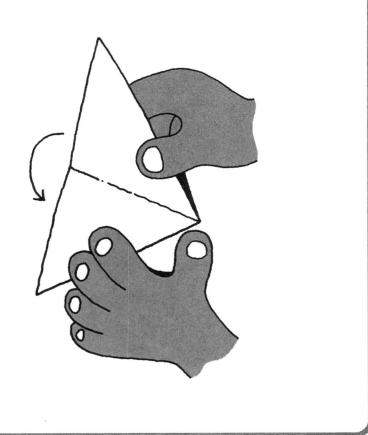

4 Intercambien sus rompecabezas. Uno a la vez, armen sus rompecabezas el uno del otro. Usen como guía el marco del triángulo de la **Marcos de rompecabezas (Home Puzzle Frames)**.

5 Armen los dos rompecabezas de triángulos para hacer un rectángulo. Usen como guía el marco de rectángulo de la **Marcos de rompecabezas (Home Puzzle Frames)**.

6 Escriban lo que piensan sobre esta actividad.

Estimado maestro:

_____

_____

De, _____

(nombre del niño)

_____

(nombre del compañero en casa)

7 Prepárense para la escuela. Escojan uno de los rompecabezas de triángulos y pónganlo en el sobre para traer de vuelta a la escuela. Hablen sobre:

- ¿Qué rompecabezas quieres llevar a la escuela?

Fold a Square

AT SCHOOL

Partners make two folds on a paper square. They unfold the square, identify shapes made by the folds, and color in the shapes.

How do we decide who will fold first?

How about if you fold first and I color first.

What shapes did we make?

Three rectangles and one square.

AT HOME

Children and their home partners do the same activity. Children bring their squares back to school.

BACK AT SCHOOL

Children make puzzles by cutting out the shapes on their paper squares from home. Partners assemble each other's puzzle.

I think you'll like putting my puzzle together.

Learning About Geometry

In this activity, children:

- recognize and describe shapes and their attributes
- combine and subdivide shapes
- explore spatial relationships.

Learning to Work Together

In this activity, children:

- share the work
- help each other.

Mathematical Vocabulary

square   cuadrado

trapezoid   trapezoide

AT SCHOOL

Get Ready

Prepare materials:

- A copy of the **At Home** activity, with the return date written on it, for each child

- An 8"x 8" paper square for each child, attached to the **At Home** activity

- Enough cutout triangles from "Triangles 3," p. 203, for half of the class to have one triangle each and a few for **Make Connections**

- Enough shapes cut out from "Other Shapes," p. 204, for half of the class to have one shape each and a few for **Make Connections**

- A few 8"x 8" paper squares for each pair and for modeling

- Crayons for each pair

Literature Link
Bear in a Square by Stella Blackstone (Barefoot Books, 1998). Introduce the activity with this book to help children find shapes inside other shapes. (optional)
Note: You may want to use the correct mathematical term *rhombus* in place of *diamond* while reading this book.

Teacher Tip
If children are not familiar with the trapezoid, you may want to introduce the shape and its name.

Make Connections

Whole Class

1. Show and discuss some of the triangles from "Triangles 3," and some of the shapes from "Other Shapes." Discuss:

    (?) What shape is this? How do you know?

    (?) What do you notice about the [trapezoid] **and the** [rectangle]? **How are they the same? How are they different?**

    (¿) ¿Qué figura es ésta? ¿Cómo lo saben?

    (¿) ¿Qué notan sobre el [trapezoide] *y el* [rectángulo]? *¿En qué se parecen? ¿En qué se diferencian?*

2. Randomly distribute the shapes so that half of the class has triangles and the other half has other shapes. Explain that children will walk around the room and find a partner who has a different shape. Ask:

    (?) If [Ana] **has a** [triangle] **and** [Nathan] **has a** [rectangle], **can they be partners? Why?**

(?) **How can we be responsible as we walk around the room?**

(¿) *Si [Ana] tiene [un triángulo] y [Nathan] tiene [un rectángulo], ¿pueden ser compañeros? ¿Por qué?*

(¿) *¿Cómo podemos ser responsables mientras caminamos por la clase?*

3. Have children find their partners.

4. First in pairs, then as a class, discuss:

(?) **What do you know about your two shapes?**

(?) **What is the same about your two shapes? What is different?**

(¿) *¿Qué saben sobre sus dos figuras?*

(¿) *¿En qué se parecen sus dos figuras? ¿En qué se diferencian?*

Whole Class in Pairs

Teacher Tip
Use a strategy such as *Turn to Your Partner* to give all children a chance to think and talk about the questions.

Explain and Model the Activity

1. Show a paper square and discuss:

(?) **What is the name of this shape? How is a square different from a triangle?**

(?) **How could you fold this square to make some shapes with the folds?** (Have a child demonstrate.) **What shapes did [Susan] make with the folds? How do you know? What's another way to fold the square to make some shapes?**

(¿) *¿Cómo se llama esta figura? ¿En qué se diferencian un cuadrado de un triángulo?*

(¿) *¿Cómo pueden doblar un cuadrado para formar figuras con las partes que se forman al doblarlo? (Demostración de un niño). ¿Qué figuras hizo [Susan] con sus partes? ¿Cómo lo saben? ¿De qué otra manera podemos doblar el cuadrado para hacer algunas figuras?*

Activity Directions

Pairs will:

- make two folds on a paper square
- unfold the square and color each shape in the square a different color
- talk about the shapes they made
- write their names on the square.

2. Choose a child to be your partner and demonstrate the activity as you explain the directions one at a time. As you model, ask your partner:

> **How can we share the work? Is that fair? Why do you think so?**

> **What shapes did we make with our folds? How do you know?**

> *¿Cómo podemos compartir el trabajo? ¿Es eso justo? ¿Por qué creen eso?*

> *¿Qué figuras formamos con nuestros pliegues? ¿Cómo lo saben?*

Pair Work

1. Distribute materials to each pair.

2. Have pairs do the activity. Circulate and talk with them about their work and their thinking:

Children Working in Pairs

> **What shape do you think you will make with that fold? What shape did you make?**

> **How are you helping each other?**

> *¿Qué figura piensan formar con ese pliegue? ¿Qué figura formaron?*

> *¿Cómo se están ayudando?*

Report and Reflect

1. First in pairs, then as a class, discuss:

Whole Class in Pairs

> **What shapes did you make? How do you know? Who else made that shape? Did you fold your paper the same way? What happened?**

> **How can you fold the square to make at least one [rectangle]? Is there another way to make a [rectangle]? How?**

> **How did you share the work? Would you do it that way again? Why?**

(¿) *¿Qué figuras formaron? ¿Cómo lo saben? ¿Quién más formó esa figura? ¿Doblaron su papel de la misma manera? ¿Qué pasó?*

(¿) *¿Cómo pueden doblar el cuadrado para formar al menos un [rectángulo]? ¿Hay alguna otra manera de formar un [rectángulo]? ¿Cuál?*

(¿) *¿Cómo compartieron el trabajo? ¿Lo harían otra vez de esa manera? ¿Por qué?*

Prepare for Success at Home

Whole Class

1. Show and explain the **At Home** activity. Explain that children and their home partners will make two folds on a paper square, then color and discuss the shapes. Ask:

   (?) **What will you and your home partner do?**

   (¿) *¿Qué van a hacer tu compañero en casa y tú?*

2. Explain when children are to bring their **At Home** activities and folded squares back to class and that they will be used to make puzzles. Discuss:

   (?) **Why is it important to bring your square back to class? What helps you remember to bring things back to class?**

   (¿) *¿Por qué es importante traer a clase su cuadrado? ¿Qué les ayuda a recordar que tienen que traer cosas a clase?*

BACK AT SCHOOL

Get Ready

1. Collect and review the **At Home** activities.

2. Check that each square has the child's name on it.

3. Determine how you will select partners.

4. Prepare materials:

- A 9" x 9" sheet of construction paper or tag board for each child

- Scissors for each pair

- Glue for each pair

Discuss the At Home Activity

1. Select pairs and have partners sit together. Return the **At Home** activities and paper squares to children. Discuss:

   Whole Class in Pairs

   (?) **Who was your home partner? How did you help each other do the work?**

   (?) **What shapes did you and your home partner make with the folds? How do you know?**

   (¿) *¿Quién fue su compañero en casa? ¿Cómo se ayudaron a hacer la tarea?*

   (¿) *¿Qué figuras formaron tú y tu compañero en casa al doblar las figuras? ¿Cómo lo saben?*

2. Have partners:

   Children Working in Pairs

   - cut out their squares on the folds to make puzzle pieces

   - exchange puzzles and assemble each other's puzzle on the tag board or construction paper

   - glue the puzzles to the tag board or construction paper.

3. Have pairs show their puzzles to the class. Discuss:

   Whole Class in Pairs

   (?) **How did you figure out how to put the pieces back together? How did you help each other?**

   (?) **What shapes are in your puzzle? How do you know?**

   (?) **Show us pieces of your puzzle that are** [triangles].

Teacher Tip
Choose a strategy such as *Pair Q and A* to help children learn to ask a partner questions.

¿ *¿Cómo averiguaron cómo armar las piezas? ¿Cómo se ayudaron?*

¿ *¿Qué figuras hay en su rompecabezas? ¿Cómo lo saben?*

¿ *Muéstrennos piezas de su rompecabezas que sean [triángulos].*

Extend the Experience

- Use the assembled puzzle squares to make a class quilt or math bulletin board display.

- Have each child create postcard puzzle greetings to send to a family member, school buddy, or friend. Ask them to write a message or draw a picture on a square piece of paper. Have them cut the square twice, put the pieces into an envelope, and deliver the puzzle to the recipient to assemble.

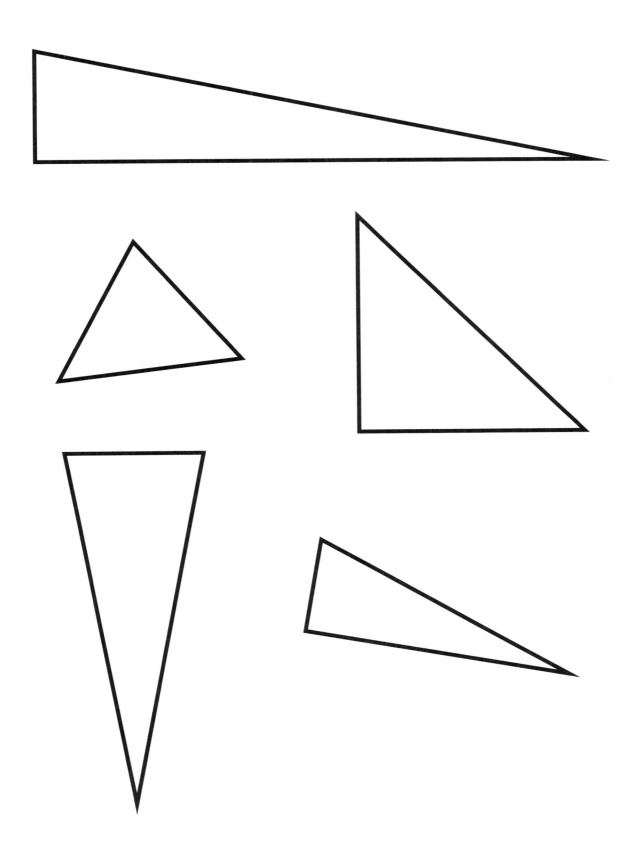

Triangles 3

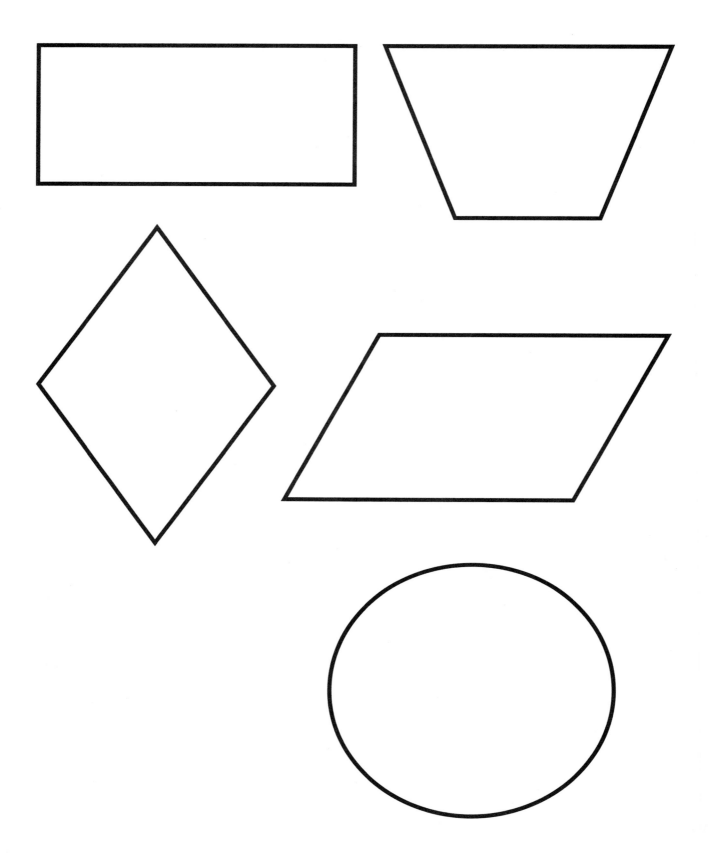

Other Shapes

Fold a Square

Dear Family,

Our class is learning about geometry. We folded paper squares to see the shapes the folds made. This helped us learn to:

- understand that shapes can be made from or divided into other shapes
- use math words such as *rectangle, sides,* and *vertices* (corners).

In this activity, you will make two folds on a paper square and color the shapes made by the folds. In class, we will use the paper square to make a puzzle.

❶ Collect the things you need.
- A pencil, pen, or crayon
- The attached paper square

❷ Talk about folding a square at school.

❸ Do the activity.

- Fold the paper square two times.

- Unfold the square.

- Color the shapes using a different color or design for each shape.
- Talk about the shapes made by the folds.

MathLinks At Home Activity

4 In the space below, draw or write about the shapes you made.

5 Write your thoughts about this activity.

Dear Teacher:

_____

_____

_____

From, _____

(child's name)

_____

(home partner's name)

6 Get ready for school. Write the child's name on the back of the square. **Talk about:**

• How many shapes did we make?

• What can we do to make sure the paper square gets back to school?

Doblar un cuadrado

Estimada familia:

Nuestra clase está aprendiendo acerca de la geometría. Doblamos cuadrados de papel para ver las figuras que formaban los pliegues. Esto nos ayudó a:

- entender que las figuras se pueden formar con otras figuras o que se pueden dividir en otras figuras
- usar palabras matemáticas como *rectángulo, lados y vértices* (esquinas).

En esta Actividad en casa, ustedes van a hacer dos pliegues en un cuadrado de papel y van a colorear las figuras formadas por los pliegues. En clase, usaremos el cuadrado de papel para hacer un rompecabezas.

① Reúnan las cosas que necesiten.
- Un lápiz, una pluma o un creyón
- El cuadrado de papel incluido

② Hablen sobre el cuadrado que doblaron en la escuela.

Cuéntame acerca de las figuras que formaste en la escuela cuando doblaste un cuadrado.

Formamos cuatro cuadrados pequeños con dos pliegues.

③ Hagan la actividad.

- Doblen el cuadrado de papel dos veces.

- Desdoblen el cuadrado.

- Coloreen las figuras usando un color o un diseño diferente para cada figura.

- Hablen sobre las figuras formadas por los pliegues.

4 En el espacio de abajo, dibujen o escriban sobre las figuras que formaron.

5 Escriban lo que piensan sobre esta actividad.

Estimado maestro:

_____

_____

De, _____

(nombre del niño)

(nombre del compañero en casa)

6 Prepárense para la escuela. Escriba el nombre del niño en la parte de atrás del cuadrado. Hablen sobre:

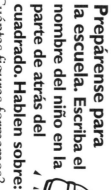

- ¿Cuántas figuras formamos?
- ¿Qué podemos hacer para estar seguros de que el cuadrado de papel vuelva a la escuela?

ADDITIONAL READING

Mathematical Development

Barron, Marlene, and Karen Romano Young. *Ready, Set, Count*. New York: John Wiley and Sons, Inc., 1995.

Fuys, David J. and Amy K. Liebov. "Geometry and Spatial Sense." *Research Ideas for the Classroom: Early Childhood Mathematics*. New York: Macmillan Publishing Co., 1993.

Geary, David C. *Children's Mathematical Development: Research and Practical Applications*. Washington, D.C.: American Psychological Association, 1994.

Jensen, Robert J., ed. *Research Ideas for the Classroom: Early Childhood Mathematics*. New York: Macmillan Publishing Company, 1993.

Kamii, Constance. *Young Children Reinvent Arithmetic: Implementation of Piaget's Theory*. New York: Teachers College Press, 1985.

Kamii, Constance. *Young Children Continue to Reinvent Arithmetic, 2nd Grade: Implications of Piaget's Theory*. New York: Teachers College Press, 1989.

Kamii, Constance. *Young Children Continue to Reinvent Arithmetic: 3rd Grade: Implications of Piaget's Theory*. New York: Teachers College Press, 1994.

Kamii, Constance and Faye Clark. "Measurement of Length: The Need for a Better Approach to Teaching." *School Science and Mathematics*, March 1997.

Kamii, Constance and Linda Joseph. "Teaching Place Value and Double-Column Addition." *Arithmetic Teacher*, National Council of Teachers of Mathematics, February 1988.

Kastner, Bernice. "Number Sense: The Role of Measurement Applications." *Arithmetic Teacher*, National Council of Teachers of Mathematics, February 1989.

Lara-Alecia, Rafael, Beverly J. Irby, and Leonel Morales-Aldana. "A Mathematics Lesson from the Mayan Civilization." *Teaching Children Mathematics*, National Council of Teachers of Mathematics, November 1998.

Mokros, Jan, Susan Jo Russell, and Karen Economopoulos. *Beyond Arithmetic: Changing Mathematics in the Elementary Classroom*. Menlo Park: Dale Seymour Publications, 1995.

National Council of Teachers of Mathematics. *Principles and Standards for School Mathematics*: Reston: NCTM, 2000.

Payne, Joseph N. and DeAnn M. Huinker. "Early Number and Numeration." *Research Ideas for the Classroom: Early Childhood Mathematics*. New York: Macmillan Publishing Co, 1993.

Piaget, Jean. *To Understand Is to Invent*. New York: Viking Press, 1973.

Ross, Sharon H. "Parts, Wholes, and Place Value: A Developmental View." *Arithmetic Teacher*, February 1989.

Secada, Walter G., Elizabeth Fennema, and Lisa Byrd Adajian, eds. *New Directions for Equity in Mathematics Education*. New York: University of Cambridge Press, 1995.

TIMMS. *Third International Mathematics and Science Study Sourcebook of 4th-Grade Findings*. Philadelphia: Mid-Atlantic Consortium for Mathematics and Science Education, 1997.

U.S. Department of Education. *Pursuing Excellence: A Study of U.S. Fourth-Grade Mathematics and Science Achievement in International Context*. (NCES 97-255) Washington, DC: U.S. Government Printing Office, 1997.

Van de Walle, John and Karen Bowman Watkins. "Early Development of Number Sense." *Research Ideas for the Classroom: Early Childhood Mathematics*. New York: Macmillan Publishing Company, 1993.

Wilson, Patricia S. and Ruth E. Rowland. "Teaching Measurement." *Research Ideas for the Classroom: Early Childhood Mathematics*. New York: Macmillan Publishing Company, 1993.

Social Development/Cooperative Classroom

Dalton, Joan and Marilyn Watson. *Among Friends : Classrooms Where Caring and Learning Prevail*. Oakland: Developmental Studies Center, 1997.

Damon, William. *The Moral Child: Nurturing Children's Natural Moral Growth*. New York: The Free Press, 1988.

Developmental Studies Center. *Blueprints for a Collaborative Classroom*. Oakland: Developmental Studies Center, 1997.

Gibbs, Jeanne. *Tribes: A New Way of Learning and Being Together*. Santa Rosa: Center Source Publications, 1995.

Hill, Susan and Ted Hill. *The Collaborative Classroom*. Portsmouth: Heinemann, Inc., 1990.

Johnson, David W., et al. *The New Circles of Learning: Cooperation in the Classroom and School*. Association for Supervision and Curriculum Development, 1994.

Kagan, Spencer. *Cooperative Learning*. San Juan Capistrano: Kagan, 1999.

McCabe, Margaret E. and Jacqueline Rhoades. *The Nurturing Classroom: Developing Thinking Skills, Self-esteem and Responsibility Through Simple Cooperation*. Phoenix: The Phoenix Group, 1990.

Moorman, Chick and Dee Dishon. *Our Classroom: We Can Learn Together*. Portage: Personal Power Press, 1986.

Trentacosta, Janet and Margaret J. Kenny, eds. *Multicultural and Gender Equity in the Mathematics Classroom: The Gift of Diversity*. Reston: National Council of Teachers of Mathematics, 1997.

Zaslavsky, Claudia. *The Multicultural Classroom: Bringing in the World*. Portsmouth: Heinemann, Inc.,1996.

Parent Involvement

American Association of School Administrators. *Building Self-Esteem*. Arlington: 1991.

American Association of School Administrators. *Getting Your Child Ready for School...and the School Ready for Your Child*. Arlington: 1992.

American Association of School Administrators. *Helping Your Child Communicate*. Arlington: 1990.

American Association of School Administrators. *Homework: Helping Students Achieve*. Arlington: 1985.

American Association of School Administrators. *Parenting Skills: Bringing Out the Best in Your Child*. Arlington: 1989.

American Association of School Administrators. *101 Ways Parents Can Help Students Achieve*. Arlington: 1991.

Carger, Chris Liska. *Of Borders and Dreams: A Mexican-American Experience of Urban Education*. New York: Teachers College Press, 1996.

Coates, Grace Dávila and Jean Kerr Stenmark. *Family Math for Young Children*. Berkeley: Lawrence Hall of Science, The Regents of the University of California, 1997.

Decker, Larry E., et al. *Teacher's Manual for Parent and Community Involvement*. Fairfax: National Community Education Association, 1997.

Henderson, Anne T. and Nancy Berla, eds. *A New Generation of Evidence: The Family is Critical to Student Achievement*. Washington, DC: National Committee for Citizens in Education, 1994.

Kenschaft, Patricia C. *Math Power: How to Help Your Child Love Math, Even If You Don't*. Reading: Addison-Wesley, 1997.

McNamara, Cathy, Mary Yuen, and Carol Hollingworth. *The Backpack Homework Book Math*. San Diego: Teachers Resource Center, 1997.

Mokros, Janice R. and TERC. *Beyond Facts & Flashcards: Exploring Math With Your Kids*. Portsmouth: Heinemann, 1996.

Polonsky, Lydia, et al. *Math for the Very Young: A Handbook of Activities for Parents and Teachers*. New York: John Wiley and Sons, Inc., 1995.

U.S. Department of Education. *Learning Partners: A Guide to Educational Activities for Families*. Washington, D.C., 1997.

U.S. Department of Education. *Fathers' Involvement in Their Children's Schools*. Washington, D. C., 1997.

U.S. Department of Education. *Helping Your Child With Homework*. Washington, D. C., 1995.

U.S. Department of Education. *Strong Families, Strong Schools: Building Community Partnerships for Learning*. Washington, D. C., 1994.

Valdés, Guadalupe. *Con Respeto: Bridging the Distances Between Culturally Diverse Families and Schools*. New York: Teachers College Press, 1996.

TEACHER SUPPORT MATERIALS FROM DEVELOPMENTAL STUDIES CENTER

●●●

Among Friends: Classrooms Where Caring and Learning Prevail

In classroom vignettes and conversations with teachers, this 210-page book provides concrete ideas for building caring learning communities in elementary school classrooms. With a focus on how the ideas of the research-based Child Development Project (CDP) play out in practice, Australian educator Joan Dalton and former CDP Program Director Marilyn Watson take us into classrooms where teachers make explicit how they promote children's intellectual, social, and ethical development. A chapter on theory and research provides a coherent rationale for the approach teachers demonstrate.

The Among Friends Package includes the book, 4 video cassettes visiting 8 classrooms, the Collegial Study Guide, the Teacher Educator Guide, and a packet of 20 teacher reflection guides.

AfterSchool KidzLit (Grades K-8)
An academic enrichment program for out-of-school sites and summer sessions, KidzLit helps children develop a love of reading while building literacy and character. Easy-to-use, field-tested facilitator guides for 100 involving books provide youth workers, volunteers, and teachers with good ideas and techniques for discussion, games, writing, drama, art, and "cool words" in read-aloud and book club sessions.

AfterSchool KidzLit is packaged in sets of ten guides and books per grade-range grouping (K-3, 3-5, 6-8) with a "Quick Tips" leader's manual. Additional copies of accompanying trade books and packages of student journals are also available separately.

AfterSchool KidzLit On-Site Training Kit
This package is designed for use in addition to or instead of in-person staff development for individuals or small groups. Six modules and four videotapes cover ways to launch the program, read aloud or set up group reading, build vocabulary, facilitate discussions, and help kids connect the stories to their own real life experiences and interests. The kit also includes a sample book, guide, "Quick Tips," and journal.

AfterSchool Math
Two separate books, each appropriate for grades K-2, offer games and story guides to help children develop key mathematical skills. Providing collaborative rather than competitive activities, the games and story guides also build children's abilities to make fair decisions, be responsible, and encourage and support each other. The books can be used flexibly in out-of-school and summer sessions, tutoring programs, math or game clubs, free-choice time, and as structured activities. Blackline masters and reproducible game boards are included. Children's trade books to accompany the book of story guides are sold separately.

At Home in Our Schools

The 136-page book focuses on schoolwide activities that help elementary school educators and parents create caring school communities. It includes ideas about leadership, step-by-step guidelines for 15 activities, and reproducible planning resources and suggestions for teachers. The 12-minute overview video is designed for staff meetings and parent gatherings to create support for a program of whole-school activities. The 48-page study guide structures a series of organizing meetings for teachers, parents, and administrators. The At Home in Our Schools Package includes the book, the overview video, and the Collegial Study Guide. (Also available separately.)

Blueprints for a Collaborative Classroom

This 192-page "how-to" collection of partner and small-group activities is organized into 25 categories that range from quick partner interviews to complex research projects. Over 250 activity suggestions are included for all elementary grades. In addition, Fly on the Wall vignettes offer insights from real classrooms.

The Blueprints for a Collaborative Classroom Package includes the book, an overview video, 3 video cassettes visiting 6 classrooms, the Collegial Study Guide, the Teacher Educator Guide, and a packet of 20 teacher reflection guides.

Choosing Community: Classroom Strategies for Learning and Caring

In 9 videotaped presentations, author and lecturer Alfie Kohn describes pivotal choices that promote community and avoid coercion and competition in classrooms. A 64-page facilitator's guide for use in staff development accompanies the presentations, which include such topics as "The Case Against Competition," "The Consequences of 'Consequences,'" "The Trouble with Rewards," and "Beyond Praise and Grades." The package also includes Kohn's influential book Punished by Rewards: The Trouble with Gold Stars, Incentive Plans, A's, Praise and Other Bribes.

Company in Your Classroom

This 104-page book supports the master teacher in building a learning relationship with the student teacher. Useful tools and checklists supplement material on first meetings, involving the student teacher in the classroom community, exchanging information about the children, student teacher observation, coaching, and developing competencies. In candid interviews, experienced and student teachers talk openly about the challenges and successful approaches to communication, support, and understanding.

Homeside Activities (Grades K–6)

Seven separate collections of activities by grade level help teachers, parents, and children communicate. Each 128-page collection has an introductory overview, 18 reproducible take-home activities in both English and Spanish, and suggestions for integrating the activities into the classroom. The 12-minute English overview video is for parent gatherings and can be used in staff development (as can a 31-minute version). A separate Spanish overview video is specifically designed for parent meetings. The 48-page study guide structures a series of teacher meetings for collegial study.

The Homeside Activities Package includes 6 books (one each grades K–5), the overview video, the study guide, and a 31-minute video visiting 3 classrooms and parents working at home with their children. (Also available separately, as are the grade 6 book and the Spanish overview tape.)

MathLinks (Grades K-2)

Each of three grade-level teacher-resource books is designed to help children connect their mathematical and social learning at school and at home through lessons and take-home activities. Enjoyable explorations in number, measurement, and geometry give children practice with curriculum skills and concepts, build their ability to work with others, and involve parents in their children's learning.

Number Power (Grades K–6)

Each of nine 192-page teacher resource books offers 3 replacement units (8–12 lessons per unit) that foster students' mathematical and social development. Students collaboratively investigate problems, develop their number sense, enhance their mathematical reasoning and communication skills, and learn to work together effectively. (Grades K, 1, 4, 5, and 6 have one volume each; grades 2 and 3 have two volumes each.)

Reading, Thinking & Caring: Literature-Based Reading (Grades K–3)

A children's literature program to help students love to read, think deeply and critically, and care about how they treat themselves and others. Teaching units are available for over 100 classic, contemporary, and multicultural titles. Each 3- to 10-day unit includes a take-home activity in both English and Spanish to involve parents. Also available are grade-level sets and accompanying trade books.

Reading for Real: Literature-Based Reading (Grades 4–8)

A literature-based program to engage the student's conscience while providing interesting and important reading, writing, speaking, and listening experiences. Teaching units are available for 120 classic, contemporary, and multicultural titles, and each 1- to 3-week unit includes a take-home activity to involve parents. Also available are grade-level sets and accompanying trade books.

SIPPS (Systematic Instruction in Phoneme Awareness, Phonics, and Sight Words)

This three-level program by John Shefelbine and Katherine K. Newman teaches decoding efficiently and effectively, through fast-paced lessons with substantial student interaction. It is developmentally appropriate for kindergarten through third grade, covering single-syllable words in the Beginning and Extension levels and polysyllabic decoding in the Challenge Level. All three levels can be used as intervention programs for older, struggling readers, and it is also appropriate for English learners.

Kits at the three levels include various combinations of teacher lesson books; wall cards or charts; hand-held sight-word, spelling-sound, phonics, and sight-syllable cards; story books; and poster-size story charts.

That's My Buddy! Friendship and Learning Across the Grades

The 140-page book is a practical guide for two buddy teachers or a whole staff. It draws on the experiences of teachers from DSC's Child Development Project schools across the country in building relationships through cross-grade activities. The 12-minute overview video is designed for use at staff meetings to enhance interest in a schoolwide buddies program. The 48-page study guide structures a series of teacher meetings for collegial study and support once a buddies program is launched.

The Collegial Study Package includes the book, the overview video, and the study guide. (Also available separately.)

Ways We Want Our Class to Be: Class Meetings That Build Commitment to Kindness and Learning

The 116-page book describes how to use class meetings to build a caring classroom community and address the academic and social issues that arise in the daily life of the elementary school classroom. In addition to tips on getting started, ground rules, and facilitating the meetings, 14 guidelines for specific class meetings are included. The 20-minute overview video introduces 3 kinds of class meetings. The 48-page study guide helps structure a series of teacher meetings for collegial study. In-depth video documentation shows 7 classrooms where students are involved in planning and decision making, checking in on learning and behavior, and problem solving.

The Collegial Study Package includes the book, the overview video, the study guide, and 99 minutes of video documenting 7 classrooms. (Also available separately.)

Professional development is offered on many of the programs and materials described above. For further information, please contact the Developmental Studies Center at (800) 666-7270 or visit our website: *www.devstu.org*.